The 30 Day Challenge Book: 500 Ideas to Inspire Your Life

CLARE HUDSON

DISCLAIMER

This book is designed to provide a wide range of 30 day challenges that may not be suitable for everyone. The author is not offering psychological, health, financial and other professional services advice. The ideas featured are for informational and entertainment purposes only and are not substitutes for professional, medical, financial, health or psychological advice. When you choose your 30 day challenges, you are required to source more detailed information to assist you and make sure that your challenges are suitable for you.

If you are in doubt as to whether a 30 day challenge is suitable or you have specific health requirements or allergies, please consult or seek the advice of an appropriately qualified or competent professional person who can assist you, such as your doctor, healthcare provider, psychologist or financial adviser. You are solely responsible for your own actions, choices and the results of your 30 day challenges. Therefore, doing any of the 30 day challenges in this book are at your own risk. The author is not liable for any negative consequences or physical, psychological, emotional, financial, or commercial damages, as a result of reading this book and/ or implementing any of the 30 day challenge ideas.

For my parents who edited this book
and everyone who helped me brainstorm ideas.
Very much appreciated.

CONTENTS

Your free 30 day challenge planner chart

Access your FREE 30 day challenge planner chart through this mini URL: goo.gl/BbGBjp

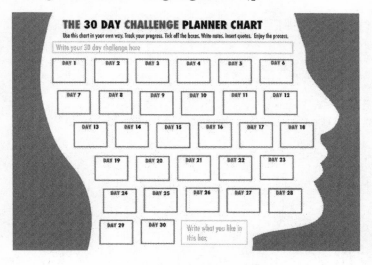

Copy this URL into your computer goo.gl/BbGBjp, download the PDF and print it out.

If you're having problems downloading it, please email me at clare@thoughtbrick.com and I can send it to you directly.

Introduction

My note to you

10 years ago, I did a Fine Art degree, but for years I felt completely uninspired to create any of my own art. It was a 30 day mandala drawing challenge that got me into making art again, thanks to Matt Cutts and his brilliant TED talk: Try something new for 30 days, which is where I first heard about 30 day challenges.

Every day I looked forward to the time I spent drawing — not for where it might lead me next or what I might get out of it at the end. The process of being in the moment and drawing every day was enough.

As an added bonus, after my 30 day challenge, I felt inspired to set up an Etsy shop with my Mum, selling yoga and nature inspired art prints designed by us both. This idea probably wouldn't have occurred to me or I wouldn't have acted on it if I hadn't started the 30 day challenge. We might not be taking over the world with our prints, but that's not the point; my heart is there; it's great to have a project with my Mum and I'm loving the process of it.

Similarly, after trying quite a few 30 days challenges myself and writing about them on my blog, this time one year ago, I set myself the challenge to write the first draft of this book in 30 days, which I managed to do — just! One year later, after lots of editing and discussions with people, the book is complete.

Whether I make sales or not, I can wholeheartedly say that I've loved every minute of the process and have tried hard to create something I think will be useful for you, that you can refer back to time and time again.

—

The point of this book isn't to tell you how to live or give you ideas only I like — it's to get you to start and do something today or at least within the week. Some of the ideas you'll love, some might not be for you, but pretty much all of them can be started straight away either for free or without spending much money. The idea is to use the resources you have already, and pick the ideas that speak to your heart.

While reading this book alone without putting anything into action won't change your life, it's my hope that you will find something in here that will make you feel excited. And through the act of doing, I hope you get the chance to reignite old passions, find enthusiasm for everyday life and develop a love for trying new things.

Before you start your 30 day challenges

You don't always need to partake in massive life altering experiences, around the world adventures or make drastic lifestyle changes to your routine to make a significant difference to your life. Although I'll never say no to an adventure, I'd like to think that long term change comes from your outlook on life. It's not necessarily where you are, but what you do with your time there.

What I like about 30 day challenges is that you can make a massive difference to your life without having to spend loads of money, relocate or wait until the time is right. The majority of the 30 day challenge ideas I've written about in this book can be done anywhere — some of them for as little as five minutes a day, without spending any money or needing lots of equipment.

Free 30 day challenge planner chart
Go to goo.gl/BbGBjp to access it

Before you start any of the 30 day challenges, you have the option of downloading and printing off your free 30 day challenge planner chart, which you can access via the following URL: goo.gl/BbGBjp

This is optional and you can start any of the challenges without it, but I thought it would be useful to have something so you can record results, plan out your challenge, or write daily notes to yourself to keep going. Be creative and use it as an additional tool to help you stay motivated.

How to use your 30 day challenge planner chart

The 30 day challenge planner chart is yours to use in any way you want, but here are some suggestions for how you might use it.

- For fitness challenges, record what you did each day to exercise, plan out your fitness schedule — gradually increasing the intensity of your challenge, or write down the number of steps you walked each day.

- For food challenges, plan out your meals for the month.

- If you're trying to increase your vocabulary, write a different word you'd like to learn on each square and spend a day trying to use that word in your conversations with people.

- For gratitude challenges, write one thing you're grateful for each day.

- For money challenges, write how much you made or saved.

- For any of the challenges, write a sentence in each square to document your thoughts and how you felt at the end of each day.

You can print out as many of these charts as you like for your personal use, but it might be easier to do one challenge at a time. To help you stay motivated, you could also get others to do 30 day challenges with you, or get someone to hold you accountable. Although most of the challenges can be started right now, you may like to give yourself a week to prepare.

How to use this book

I encourage you to dip in and out of this book rather than reading it from front to back, unless you want to of course. I've divided it up into categories but if you're unsure where to start, you could begin by turning to a chapter you like the sound of and picking a challenge at random. As you progress with your 30 day challenge, I encourage you to write notes to record your progress, along with any new ideas that spring to mind.

500 30 day challenges have been divided up into six main categories.

- Self improvement, inner life and meditation 30 day challenges

- Recreational, art and creative 30 day challenges

- Home life, Professional life and finance 30 day

challenges

- Intellectual and educational 30 day challenges

- Social, relationships and kindness 30 day challenges

You can also go straight to the **30 day challenge A-Z** at the back of this book which lists all 500 challenges alphabetised by the category the challenge is listed under.

3 helpful tips for getting the most out of your 30 day challenge

1. Love the process

The biggest lesson 30 day challenges have taught me, is to love the process. I'm not against goal setting, but many of us live in a world that focuses only on goals and deadlines. I think, if we can learn to love the steps in between, we can be much happier, rather than hopping from milestone to milestone and forgetting the little things that make up most of our lives.

2. Trust your intuition

Some of these challenges could change your life, others might be completely unsuitable for you — the idea is to use your intuition and find what feels right for you. If you're in any doubt as to whether a challenge is suitable for you or not, seek advice from your healthcare provider, doctor or those close to you.

3. Be resourceful

For me, resourcefulness is about looking around at what you have already and doing things. These challenges are designed to help you try new things in a resourceful and creative way, without having to spend lots of money.

Why this book isn't about breaking bad habits

According to this 2009 study, How are habits formed: Modelling habit formation in the real world[1], it actually takes 66 days to break bad habits.

The ideas featured in this book aren't supposed to help you kick bad habits necessarily — they're designed to give you inspiration, help you to start something new, or give you the opportunity to sample something you've never done before.

Therefore, I encourage you to look at the 30 day challenges in this book, not as a way to break bad habits, but as a tool to help you to love the present moment for what it is. Who knows what new opportunities, inspiration and ideas might come out of your 30 day challenge as a bonus. The only rule is: do something every day for 30 days. The rest is up to you.

Let's get started

Pick your 30 day challenge — do it every day for 30 days — love the process and see what happens next.

Health, food and fitness 30 day challenges

Exercise and fitness
Food and drink
Beauty, pampering and body image
Sleep

Exercise and fitness
30 day challenges

1. Train for a triathlon or running event

Set yourself up a 30 day training plan and fit triathlon training around your daily routine. It'll probably take you longer than a month to train for a marathon, but if the thought is daunting, running every day for 30 days could give you a boost in confidence as you'll see how much further you can run each time.

2. Dance every day — whether you're good at it or not

This isn't about memorising moves. Put some music on and just dance freely for 10 minutes every day without caring what you look like. It's one of the most freeing things you can do.

3. Teach yourself to handstand

I'm doing this at the moment and admittedly it's taking me much longer than a month, but starting this as a 30 day challenge helped to make this a habit and I've noticed a massive improvement. Find a programme that's right for your fitness level and see how you get on. Remember to never strain or push your body. If you're looking for a book, you could start with *How to do a Handstand*[2].

4. Do 10,000 steps a day

I used a FitBit[3] to track my steps, but it might not be necessary. From my own experience, it took approximately an hour and 15 mins to do 10,000 steps. Walking could help you to get fitter, build stamina and give you a healthier heart.[4] Perhaps this one is for you if the thought of starting an exercise regime is daunting.

5. Try a home workout

Decide how long you want your exercise routine to be, find a workout schedule created by an exercise professional that's suitable for your level of fitness, and get working out. Look for something that works your whole body — you don't want to overwork or strain a part of yourself by pushing yourself too much with just one thing.

6. Go for morning walks in silence

There's something incredibly therapeutic about silent walks — whether you're alone or in a group. If you can manage it, wake up before sunrise and walk as the day lightens. this is a really beautiful way to start the day.

7. Try yoga

Many yoga studios offer unlimited yoga classes for 30 days at a significantly reduced discount, which could be worth trying — especially if you're unsure which style of yoga you prefer. Alternatively, *Yoga with Adriene* has an online yoga programme lasting 30 days which you can access on YouTube.

8. Cycle to work

If you do this — seek out cycle paths and stay safe. I have a really old bike from the 50s that doesn't go very fast so I never really get sweaty when I cycle, but riding it is still more healthy than taking a train, plus it's a much more pleasant way to get around London in the summer.

9. Go on a 30 day bike ride and see how far you get

I haven't personally done this, but love the idea. If you've got a month to spare, you could set out and cycle a little further each day, either camping or staying in cheap hostels along the way. This is also a really good way to explore your country a bit more.

10. Take up a new exercise or martial art you can learn from YouTube

If you don't want to join a class, there are loads of good online videos you can try. While I prefer yoga, I did try Tai Chi for a month. Other things to consider could be learning to use a contact ball, juggling or karate.

11. Spend time upside down or with your legs up the wall

There are loads of benefits to spending a bit of time upside down or practising yoga inversions[5], but for me, I always feel mentally lighter after practising them. Just make sure you warm up properly first and never push or force your body to do something it's not ready for. If you don't know how to do these inversions, don't attempt them unless you've been taught safely and directly by a teacher first. Alternatively, you could try the more restorative yoga asana of Legs up the wall pose[6].

Food and drink
30 day challenges

12. Drink a pint of hot water with lemon and ginger first thing in the morning

Add or subtract the lemon and ginger. I do this one every morning, and feel so much better for it. As for the straight hot water drinking, my friend Connie got me into this. It feels so much better than drinking cold water in the winter.

13. Cook with turmeric

I bought this fantastic spice and recipe book called *Discovering the Spices of Morocco* whilst I was in Morocco. It lists all the medicinal and health properties for certain spices. According to the book, turmeric has many benefits including helping to prevent cancer, improving digestion and combatting stress[7]. I now try to add at least half a teaspoon a day to my cooking.

14. Drink green tea (high in antioxidants)[8] every morning

I did this for a while and felt really healthy. You could see how you feel switching your regular tea or coffee for green tea. Remember green tea still has caffeine in unless you get the decaffeinated version.

15. Present your food nicely

There are probably no health benefits at all to this, but it's something I personally like to do, and it makes me enjoy my food more. There might also be some benefit to spending time on yourself in this way and making your plate look like a work of art. Give it a go and see how it feels.

16. Make spontaneous meals with limited ingredients

This is the opposite of following recipes from a cookbook, and something I love doing. Sometimes people thank me for it (I make a good nut roast) and sometimes they don't. The idea is to be creative with the ingredients you currently own or buy random ingredients that you like and make a meal with them.

17. Try out a new diet

In all honesty, I've never tried any well known diets so I

have non to personally recommend. I am also in no way, suggesting you should diet! However, if you're looking for a new diet to try, the NHS have published an article called *Top Diets Review for 2016*[9] which lists 12 diets with the pros and cons from experts. The review includes the 5:2 diet (intermittent fasting), Dukan diet, Paleo diet, and the new Atkins diet.

18. Don't drink caffeine after midday

This goes without saying if you often have trouble sleeping. Find other things such as short bursts of exercise or drinking enough water, to boost energy levels.

19. Cook a meal you've never made before

After a month you'll have cooked 30 new meals which you can later adapt and make them your own. Sometimes you can end up eating the same thing every day, which can make meals boring. There are plenty of delicious and healthy dishes you can make in as little as 10 minutes. Spend some time planning for this challenge and find 30 recipes you like the sound of that can be made easily. Gather together the ingredients for each week and start cooking.

20. Grow your own Scoby and make your own kombucha

I was first introduced to the idea of growing your own scoby and drinking kombucha by my friend Heli during my yoga teacher training in India. Scoby stands for symbiotic culture of bacteria and yeast and takes between two to four weeks to grow, so perfect for a 30 day challenge. Once you've grown your scoby you can then make the drink kombucha which supposedly has lots of health benefits[10]. There are plenty of recipes online.

21. Be aware of what you're really eating

This one is about becoming more aware of foods with misleading packaging such as drinks that look healthy but actually contain a crazy amount of sugar. If you do find any surprises, see what alternatives you can use instead that are healthier for you.

22. Try eating at different times

Eating three times a day is considered to be the norm in western culture. I'm not suggesting you drastically switch your meal schedule, but if, for example, you never eat breakfast, see what it feels like to eat it. Do some research, and see what takes your fancy.

23. Try out being a vegetarian or vegan

If you're an avid meat eater, hopefully this one will surprise you. I've eaten vegan and vegetarian for a month before and when you're not cooking with meat, it really forces you to think more carefully about flavours. To start with, you could try this out once or twice a week — just make sure you're getting all the correct nutrients if you decide to do it.

24. No eating out for 30 days

You'll save money and you'll know exactly what's gone into your food.

25. Swap unhealthy snacks for healthy ones

Try fruit, mixed nuts carrot sticks and hummus. You could try giving up one unhealthy snack at a time, such as crisps during the first week, chocolate the second etc. if it feels too much to give up all healthy snacks at once.

26. Make and eat your own fresh bread

Flour, oil, water and yeast — that's all you need. Indian flat breads are even simpler if you look up some recipes.

27. Train yourself to like foods you don't usually have a taste for

I desperately wanted to like olives as a child because I thought they made people look sophisticated. I kept trying them until I liked them and now I love them. Maybe you could see if you can also train yourself to like a food you usually wouldn't want to eat. Some psychologists believe that there are certain things we can do to change our tastes[11]. Why not find out for yourself.

28. Invent a new food or drink recipe

If you're into cooking, make it your mission to invent something new each day — for any meal. Once when I had a cold, I mixed together loads of ginger, honey, lemon, sage, cloves and some other herbs I knew were good for the immune system. Similarly, you could do the same with smoothie drinks.

29. Eat at least five pieces of fruit and veg every day

It's the NHS's recommended amount[12]. To make it easier, experiment with fruit and veg drinks, aim to have at least one piece of fruit or veg with every meal and swap unhealthy snacks for healthy ones.

30. Eat garlic and ginger

Garlic and ginger have anti-inflammatory properties, are supposedly good for fighting infections[13] and they go well with so many different dishes. Save time by crushing up loads of garlic and ginger and keeping it in a jar in your fridge.

31. Cook lunches for the week ahead on Sunday

You'll save money and probably eat healthier. Just stock up

on Tupperware and cook a selection of 3-5 different meals to freeze for the week ahead.

32. Eat colourful meals

This one's just my preference — I love seeing a variety of colours on my plate. It makes me enjoy my food so much more.

33. Slow down your eating

You will be able to taste your food better and you can practise mindfulness while you eat and hopefully enjoy your meal a whole lot more. Chewing your food properly may also help with digestion[14].

34. Think good thoughts when you eat

During my second yoga teacher training, this was one of things I was taught. According to ancient yogis, the thoughts you have when you eat have an impact on your state of mind, which is why it's best to eat when you're in the right state of mind.

Beauty, pampering and body image 30 day challenges

35. Work on creating a positive self image

We live in a world that often makes women feel inadequate about their bodies. This is a bit of a vague one I know, and could well take longer than a month, but you could start with little things such as ditching magazines that make you feel bad and doing other small things that are kind to yourself. It could even be as simple as limiting the amount of negative self talk you might have towards your body.

36. Ditch gossip magazines
I'm not saying they're evil, but if you consume celebrity gossip daily, experiment going cold turkey on it for a month and see how you feel afterwards. What else could you read or learn instead?

37. Steam your face
I love doing this in winter. Just fill up a bowl of hot water, add a few drops of essential oil (optional), put a towel over your head, and let your face feel clean and refreshed. Steaming according to Livestrong has supposed anti-ageing benefits and could help to improve your circulation[15].

38. Have cold showers
It might feel horrible at first, but I love a quick cold shower after my hot one. It really helps to wake me up in the morning, and there are additional benefits such as relieving stress, increasing your alertness and improving circulation[16]. However, go easy on the shower control — when I was back at my parents I accidentally broke theirs!

39. Use coconut oil
I use coconut oil every night before I go to bed and feel that it helps my skin a lot — more so than expensive moisturising creams. It's cheap and can also be used on the rest of your body as a body oil and as a mouthwash.

40. Ditch some of your beauty products
If you're heavily reliant on your eyelash curlers, straighteners, foundation… experiment giving it all up for a month. If it's too hard, select just a few beauty products to stop using. Giving up certain products up might help you to only use them when you want to as opposed to because you think you need it. Ditching foundation for a month helped me with

this one. I didn't plan to give it up for good, I just wanted to feel more comfortable leaving the house without any on.

41. Spend up to five minutes looking into your own eyes in the mirror

This one was a suggestion from my friend Lily. The idea is to open yourself up to yourself, make contact with your soul, feel beautiful (because you are) and accept yourself fully for who you are.

42. Don't look in the mirror

This will probably be hard to do unless you live permanently in a tree house or at a festival. It was a suggestion from my brother Mike who lives in a van. Perhaps this one is for you if you consistently check yourself out in shop windows, hand mirrors etc.

43. Use luxurious ethical products that make you feel good

This was a suggestion from my Mum. You don't have to excessively splash out for this one, but try simple things like using better quality soaps and shower gel that don't contain harsh chemicals and are good for the environment.

44. Go make-up free

I love wearing make-up, but for my first ever job, I used to put make-up on other people and had to come into work wearing at least five items of make-up. When I didn't wear any people would say I looked tired, even if I'd had plenty of sleep. Try going more natural for a bit and feel beautiful without it.

45. Try out different make-up techniques

If you always wear make-up in the same way, consider getting a friend to do your make-up in a new way. Maybe wear less or more for a month and observe how you feel.

46. Stop sleeping with your make-up on

I'm a big believer in this one. It feels horrible waking up with the previous days mascara on and it's not good for your skin. I use coconut oil the night before to take my make-up off.

47. Massage your feet for two minutes every night before bed

Your feet carry you around all day. Treat them to a massage before you go to bed. Once a week, after putting moisturiser on your feet, you could also sleep in socks. It might not feel overly comfortable, but your skin will feel really soft when you wake up.

48. Gently massage under and around your eyes

Lightly massaging or gentle tapping the skin around my eyes has been something I've naturally done since I was 17, to help my eyes look more awake. Although there are lots of massage tutorials online, you could try the DIY Magic Eye Massage routine by Oskia, London, which takes into account specific acupressure points[17].

49. Try wearing natural deodorant

I've made my own natural deodorant before using coconut oil, baking soda, essential oils and arrow root. There are, however, lots of different recipes you can try. Make sure you do follow a recipe to make sure you get the quantities right. Bustle published an article on wearing natural deodorant called *Is Natural Deodorant Better? I Tried An Aluminum-Free Product For A Week, And It Wasn't The Pits[18]*.

50. Learn to love yourself just a little bit more each day

———

You deserve to treat yourself well. Be aware of negative self-talk and try to say and think kinder things instead. Hold yourself well. Do things that make you feel good and reflect on self-love for a month.

51. Reorganise your wardrobe and wear a new outfit

Without realising you can probably do a lot more than you think with the clothes in your wardrobe, without having to pay a fortune for new clothes. Try to wear a combination you've never worn before every day for a week. You can always repeat the combinations for the rest of the 30 days. If you're struggling, get friends to help you match things together you wouldn't normally consider.

52. Floss

Your teeth and gums will thank you for it and it really isn't time consuming. If it's proving to be really hard, you could start by flossing just one tooth and work your way up each day[19].

53. Hold yourself well

You don't need to sit rigidly straight — just feel relaxed and comfortable with yourself. After I've done yoga asanas and meditation, I feel I can move a lot more freely, as if I'm somehow lighter on my feet and carrying less baggage. Holding yourself well, just means being comfortable.

54. Try Ayurveda oil pulling

I came across this recently and thought it was really bizarre the first few times I tried it. It basically involves swilling coconut oil around in your mouth for quite a long time. It's supposed to act as a really good mouth wash, help to keep teeth clean and white and get rid of bad breath[20].

55. Stop spending so much time on your appearance

If you spend a really long time getting ready or you can't go outside without makeup, experiment by seeing what it's like to not care about these things so much. Throw on the nearest thing in your wardrobe, limit yourself to just a few or no products, and observe how this makes you feel. If this is too much, start first by putting a time limit on the amount of time it takes you to get ready in the morning. This challenge is not about giving any of the above up permanently — it's more an experiment to see how you feel. When I did this, for a lot of the time, I didn't feel good, but it helped me to rely a lot less on my appearance.

56. Wear clothes with nice fabric

Sort through your wardrobe and only wear the clothes that feel really good on your skin. Why wear things that are itchy, don't fit properly or that make you feel bad?

57. Stop shaving/ waxing your body hair

As women, many of us have been conditioned by the beauty industry to think that we have to shave, wax and pluck all hairs that aren't on our head or in the perfect arch of our eyebrows. I'm not saying go natural forever, but you could try it out for a month. Never think that you're not beautiful if you allow yourself to be natural.

58. Make a homemade skin exfoliator

I often mix olive oil with brown sugar to exfoliate my hands in the winter. I leave the mixture on for several minutes and really give my hands a good massage. I then just rinse my hands in warm water afterwards. I can honestly say, it's probably one of the best instant remedies for dry hands that I've used. If you want it to smell good, just add some essential oil or use another base oil.

59. Develop your inner confidence

This could involve combining a few of the 30 day challenges mentioned and will be different for everyone. You could think kind thoughts about yourself, hold yourself well, or spending more time feeling your inner beauty.

60. Smile

It might feel fake if you never do it, but smiling even when you don't want to is supposed to make you happier[21]. Try it for yourself and see if it makes any difference.

61. Live according to your Ayurvedic dosha type

Find out what your Ayurvedic Dosha (Vata, Pitta, Kapha) type by visiting an Ayurvedic doctor or doing one of the many free tests online. Then live accordingly to the advice given for one month.

62. Connect your skin with the earth

Maybe it's because I'm a bit of a hippy at heart, but I love walking barefoot on grass. There's something really soothing about allowing your bare skin to connect with nature, whether it's lying on sand, walking barefoot on grass or swimming in a peaceful lake. The book Earthing[22] has some interesting things to say about our planet's natural healing energy.

Sleep 30 day challenges

63. Think only good thoughts straight before bed

Lucid Dreaming teacher Andrew Holocek mentions in his Dream Sculpting[23] course that the thoughts you have just before you drop off to sleep have an impact on your dreams. Try it and see if it works for you.

64. Go to bed at 10pm and wake up at 6am

I've always felt really productive when I go to bed at 10pm and wake up at 6am. This is a good one if you often feel sluggish in the mornings or you never feel you have enough time to do everything.

65. Train yourself to lucid dream

This is one of the best things I've experienced and I highly recommend it. I gave myself 30 days to practise, although it can take as little as a few weeks or up to several months. In a lucid dream, you wake up in the dreaming state and your dreaming reality starts to feel as real as waking life. If you want to learn more, you could start by reading the book, World of Lucid Dreaming by Stephen LaBerge[24].

66. Keep a dream diary

I record my dreams to help me prepare for lucid dreaming as it's an invaluable way to help you consistently remember your dreams. Plus, it can be amusing to look back on what you've written.

67. Monitor your sleep

I did this for a week and it was quite interesting to see how well I'd slept. I wouldn't say that I have issues problems with my sleeping, but if you do, wearing a Fitbit might help you to see more clearly what's going on when you go to bed. You can find out how to track your sleep using a Fitbit here[25].

68. Try out sleeping with siestas

Once upon a time, some of us used to sleep for only four hours at a time, twice a day[26]. I've never really consistently had siestas, but I sometimes feel sleepy at around 3pm. Perhaps this way of sleeping is more natural to us and we'll actually be more refreshed as a species if we nap more.

69. No computer or mobile phone screens after sunset

We spend a large proportion of our waking lives connected to our phones, computers and other electronic devices. Try leaving the period before you go to bed or when it gets dark, technology free and see if your sleep improves. Some doctors believe that looking at bright screens after dark could be harmful to your health[27].

70. Go snooze free on your alarm

As soon as your alarm sounds, hit the off button, take a stretch and climb straight out of bed, without wasting 20 minutes in snooze. If it's hard, set your alarm to a song instead.

71. Turn your electronical devices off before bed

If you sleep in a room with flashing lights and faint buzzing, then it might seem like common sense to say that you will have a more peaceful sleep if you turn your devices off. However, *the national Sleep Foundation*[28] goes into more detail, explaining why it's necessary to turn off your electronical gadgets before you go to sleep.

72. Place lavender under your pillow

During my time in India, loud noises would often keep me up longer than usual, so I would place drops of Lavender on my pillow to help my sleep better. This, however, is not an old wives' tale. Some researchers have confirmed that when the scent of lavender is inhaled, it produces slight soothing, calming and sedative effects[29].

73. Get yourself into a bedtime routine

Unwind properly before you go to bed and you could wake up the next day feeling so much more refreshed. Having a clear routine before you sleep might help, such as drinking a hot drink, cleansing your face, putting your pajamas on or reading. I don't have any research studies to back this one up, but it's often worked for me.

74. Eat something or don't eat something before bed

I always feel a bit groggy the next day if I've eaten a big meal just before bed. However, there's evidence to support both sides[30]. Have a look at the research and find what feels right for you.

75. Read something that makes you feel good before you go to sleep

I love reading before bed and feel that this isn't something that should stop at childhood. Even if you're not a regular reader, ask for recommendations and find a book or a collection of short stories you'll enjoy reading for a month.

Self improvement, inner life and meditation 30 day challenges

Misc self improvement
Law of attraction and manifesting
Stuff to give up
Themed mood challenges
Meditation and inner life

Misc self improvement 30 day challenges

76. Keep a thought journal

If the average person has thousands of thoughts a day, what do you spend your time thinking about? If your thoughts shape your beliefs and actions, what could you do today to change what you think about? You won't capture all your thoughts in a journal, but it might help tame your monkey mind and make you more aware of what's going on in your head all day.

77. Do something out of your comfort zone

Choose one thing to do over the course of 30 days or write down 30 smaller things to do each day to get yourself out of your comfort zone. If you're stuck for ideas, get someone who knows you well to come up with some suggestions for you.

78. Celebrate small accomplishments

Break big goals into small manageable pieces, enjoy the whole process and celebrate every small accomplishment. This could be something as little as taking a minute out of your day before you go to bed, reflecting on your greatest small accomplishment for the day and feeling grateful.

79. Write down nagging thoughts on paper and thrown them away

At the end of each day, if there's anything on your mind, just write it down on a piece of paper, tear it up and let it go. It might not solve everything but it could help to ease your mind a bit. This is something I often do and find it really helpful.

80. Keep a general diary or journal

Save moments of your life to look back on and reflect in years to come. Write down your thoughts, dreams, or the things that have happened to you today. Draw, write poems or collect memorabilia to glue in.

81. Practise laughter yoga

I once took part in a laughter yoga class at a festival that involved everyone choosing an animal to imitate. We then had to laugh like that animal. You don't necessarily need to do this, but you could just spend three minutes laughing as hard as you can. Your fake laughter will soon lead to real laughter and make you feel so much better even if it feels like a stupid exercise.

82. Start that project you've been meaning to do for ages

You can make excuses, but I'm sure there's something you could do right now to make a start on your project, even if it's as simple as sending an email or writing down one thing you can do now to move you forwards in your project.

83. Write a letter or 30 line poem to your future self

What advice would you give to yourself in five, 10 or 15 years to come? I've still got some letters that were written from my younger self which are really lovely to read. For example, when I was seven, I wrote a letter advising my future self not to smoke, which I listened to. You can do this one at any age. Write a sentence a day, then place it in an envelope to read in the future.

84. Believe in magic

You don't need to be crazy to believe in magic — just be open to possibilities in life without losing your common sense. Start each day by reflecting on one thing that's really magical in your life or the world.

85. Create a new daily routine for yourself

Wake up at a new time. Eat lunch away from your desk. Spend longer eating breakfast. You don't need to do loads of things here — just pick something and see how it feels.

86. Start a happiness journal

Write down one thing every day that made you smile. It could be moments that are personal to you, things you observe or reflections on happiness in general. In times to come, you can look back on what you've written to help lift your spirits.

87. Ask people what your strengths and weaknesses are

If you want to move forwards — perhaps to start a new career, but you're not sure what in, spend some time asking people you trust what they think are your strengths and weaknesses. You can then reflect on the answers and use them to help move you forwards or in a completely new direction.

88. Take note of the excuses you make

If you're struggling to stop making excuses, observe what excuses you're making for a month and then reflect on which ones are common sense and which ones really are just excuses covering up fear to start or finish something.

89. Learn to read body language

A lot of us are able to read people to some extent, but what else might you learn if you spent a month learning all you can about body language?

90. Plan your outfits the day before

If you spend ages getting ready, this one might help. It might also allow you to think more creatively as you'll have the time to experiment teaming new items together. I did this while I was in college for a bit. It's probably one of the few times in my life when people used to consistently compliment me on my clothes.

91. Be really tidy

If you consistently leave loads of washing up in the sink, crumbs on work surfaces, and your house is always messy, try being tidy and more organised for a month and see how it feels. If you feel you don't have the time, start by giving everything a really good clean and take it from there.

92. Spend less time on household chores

Here's another one from my friend Lily. If your main excuse is that you don't have enough time to do things and then spend hours cleaning or doing random chores, perhaps see what it feels like to cut your time on these things, stop doing them altogether or get other people to help you out? What else would you do with the saved time?

93. Develop your emotional intelligence

Reflect on what emotional intelligence means to you. Try to be more aware of your own feelings when they arise, as well as those of others and learn how to manage your emotions. Read books and articles written by psychologists such as Daniel Goleman who specialises in the field of emotional intelligence. Reading *Emotional Intelligence: Why it Can Matter More Than IQ*[31] could be a good place to start.

94. Question advice you're given

Think for yourself and trust your intuition if the advice you've been given doesn't sit right with you. You don't need to get too skeptical with this one, but realise that not everything you're told, whether it's from a book, a person you respect or from a loved one, is the objective truth.

95. Speak or listen more

Do you tend to speak more than you listen or the other way around? Spend 30 days doing the opposite of what you would normally do — especially if you feel you interrupt a lot or you want to say things but feel too afraid to speak up.

96. Show your vulnerable side

I was given this advice recently and thought it was pretty good. I also remember watching a TED talk by Brené Brown called *The Power of Vulnerability*[32] which is definitely worth watching. We live in a world where we're often expected to put on a brave face and hide our weaknesses. In reality, though, I feel it's the people who feel confident enough to show their vulnerable sides, that are the strong ones. There's obviously a line between revealing all your personal details and not revealing anything of yourself.

97. Develop your common sense and ability to plan ahead

Sometimes with little tasks, I'll make things harder for myself by taking the long way around because I hadn't properly thought about it, but hopefully I'm getting a bit better with this one. If this is an issue, give yourself time to come up with plans rather than rushing ahead, and put more thought into your actions. Ask your most organised friend for tips.

98. Ditch your common sense

Just because things have always been done in a certain way, doesn't make it the best way. Here's a quote I like by Einstein: *"Common sense is a set of prejudices acquired by age 18."* I like this one because people have often told me in the past to use my common sense more, even when things seemed at the time perfectly practical.

99. See life through an artist's eye

Artists will often highlight what most people overlook. This one is about being observant, seeing beauty and noticing the little things. Make it your mission to find one interesting or beautiful thing every day. It could be a small gesture, a conversation...anything that catches your attention. How does it change the way you see the world?

100. Take time out each day to watch your thoughts play out like a film

Spend five to ten minutes every day focusing gently on the space between your eyes. Don't try to stop any thoughts, images or emotions — just watch without judgement.

101. Be totally honest — so no lying for 30 days

This one might be harder than you think, but it's a good one to observe — just so you can see how often you usually lie. Even if you don't tell big lies, how often do you tell the truth when people ask you how you are, or what about telling the truth to yourself?

102. Care less what other people think about you

I've always struggled with this one, because naturally I just want to be liked. But I've found that a good place to start is realising the difference between a heartfelt comment made by someone you love, and a throwaway comment made by someone who doesn't know you.

103. Take more notice of what others think of you

If you never listen to anyone, then maybe this one is for you. You don't need to take on board what people say, but if you listen without judgement, you can see if what people are saying carries any weight.

104. Refrain from giving your opinion

If you'd describe yourself as being a really opinionated person, perhaps choose one moment every day where you hold back and focus on listening more to others first, or understanding people's motives.

105. Give your opinion more

If you hold back because you fear what others might think or you're being too diplomatic, try truly expressing your opinion at least once a day and see how it feels.

106. Create affirmations for your life

You could do this on your way to work, during breaks or when you're waiting in queues. Some people love self-affirmations like me, but they're not for everyone. If you're confused, you could start by reading the following *Psychology Today* article, *Do Self-affirmations work? A revisit*[33].

107. Write down a positive thought first thing in the morning

Keep a notebook and pen by the side of your bed and start your day by writing down one positive thought. If you consistently wake up and feel groggy or grumpy about the day ahead, you could see if this makes a difference. A positive thought could also be something you're grateful for — anything that sets your day off to a good start. You just have to mean what you say.

108. Write down ideas for accomplishing a long-term goal

What have you always wanted to do but never have? Give yourself a month to come up with ideas and a small action plan. When you've written down enough things, is there one thing that stands out as being more important than the rest? Start accomplishing your goal by doing this thing first.

109. Do one thing each day that makes you feel inspired

Listen to a song that inspires you, watch a TED talk[34], be around people you love...select a few things to do over the course of a month or write a list of 30 different things that make you feel inspired each day and put them into action.

110. Spend each day being as 'present' as possible

It might feel boring at first, so you might want to build up to this by practising being truly present for 30 minutes every day at first. Your key here is to be fully present when you do the tasks that normally send you into autopilot.

111. Spend time in nature

If you live in a city — especially in the winter months when the world can seem greyer than usual — find a park, spend time in your garden, or drive out to the countryside.

112. Spend time with animals

I grew up with animals and always felt like there was something missing when I'd live without any animals in the house. I currently live with seven kittens which belong to my housemate and they're so adorable. If you don't have any pets, consider walking your neighbour's dog, volunteering to look after people's pets for a month, opening your home up as a mini pet hotel or visiting a local farm.

113. Make positive subliminal messages for

your computer or mirror

If the world is already full of subliminal messages, you could try writing your own personal ones that will help you in some way. I'll often set my screensaver to a short message of some sort that makes me feel good.

114. Decide to become a master at something

In the book *Outliers: The Story of Success*[35], the author suggests it takes 10,000 hours to become a master at something. However, the following article, *The 10,000 rule is wrong. How to really master a skill*[36], suggests otherwise. Perhaps you could find out firsthand how long it takes to become a master at something. It will probably take you longer than 30 days, but this could be the start and it might help you prioritise what's most important to you in your life.

115. Develop your introverted or extroverted side

Be comfortable in your own company, learn to listen to others more, and focus on your inner world for a bit. Or spend more time with people who inspire you and make you feel energised just by talking with them. I loved reading *Quiet: The Power of Introverts in a World That Can't Stop Talking*[37].

116. Don't spread your energy over too many different things

This is one of my weaknesses in that it can take me away from focusing solely on the most important thing, but at the same time, I get really enthusiastic and driven by trying new things. If you consistently spread your energy over too many things though, realise that multitasking may not be as efficient as you think it is and you could get a lot more done by focusing on one thing at a time.

117. Bring more variety into your life

When I look back on the times in my life where I was doing more new things, I perceive that period of time to have been longer than it was. When I have no variety for a while, time just seems to speed up and the days just merge into one. Make an effort each day to introduce one small thing that's different from your everyday routine. Write out 30 things using your 30 day challenge planner chart and put them into action.

118. Spend time alone

I'm not suggesting you become a hermit, but if you never spend any time alone, consider putting aside at least half an hour every day where you're alone — especially if this is something you never do. How does it make you feel?

119. Don't judge yourself for feeling a certain way

This is probably one of the most important ones in this book. Never judge yourself or feel bad for feeling a certain way. As a teenager, for example, I grew up reading magazines that said men hate jealous women. I never liked feeling jealous either, but whenever I did I would always feel guilty and try to hide it. It's a natural emotion though and I think it's important to acknowledge it and then move on.

120. Do nothing for 30 minutes a day

If you're someone who finds it hard to switch off and relax, make a real effort to do nothing for a short period each day. We live in an illusion where we think the more we do, the more we'll get done, but we have to unwind sometimes too.

121. Question yourself when you meet someone you don't like

You might have a good reason, but maybe you don't. Maybe

this person just reminds you of someone who wasn't very nice to you once or maybe you've made false assumptions. Maybe you're right. Who knows. You don't have to become best friends with this person, but questioning why you don't like someone might help. If it's a gut instinct or your intuition, the reason might become apparent later on.

122. Trust your intuition and listen to your heart

We live in a time where logic and our minds often overrule our hearts and inner voice. Spend 30 days, really making an effort to listen to what your inner self is saying to you in your everyday life. Record your thoughts in a journal.

Law of Attraction and manifesting 30 day challenges

123. Make an image board

You could make one of these in a day, but it'll be richer if you make it over the course of a month. Spend time finding images you love the look of and want to see in your life or use Pinterest. You could also create a theme for your image board. For example, if you're looking to move house, collect images of the house you'd like to live in. Once you're done, either pin your image board up on the wall or make an effort to look at it every day and feel good. Imagine that what you're seeing is already a part of your life.

124. Reflect on the Law of Attraction

Does the law of attraction work? Try out your own 30 day

The 30 Day Challenge Book: 500 Ideas to Inspire Your Life

experiment and make your own mind up. Read books on the subject, set yourself small experiments to manifest things into your life, or maybe focus on one small things you'd like to attract into your life in a 30 day period. The first ever book I read on the subject was *The Secret*[38] which I loved reading. There may not be any concrete scientific evidence to back up this school of thought, but this doesn't mean that it can't work. Make your own mind up through firsthand experience.

125. Practise creative visualisation

This one is basically daydreaming with a purpose. Whatever it is you want to accomplish or manifest, visualise what that thing will look like in your mind's eye. How do you look when the goal has been realised? What are you feeling? Who are you with? Although you can practise creative visualisation anywhere, I've often found listening to music that makes you feel uplifted helps. Just remember to let go and not become too attached to your visualisations. And if this doesn't feel right, stop doing it.

126. Practise manifesting small things

Spend 30 days using the power of visualisation along with other law of attraction techniques, trying to manifest small things into your life. You could start off really small if you're skeptical and work your way up. For example, when I did this, I set the intention on separate days to find images of snakes, lions and purple feathers in a 24-hour period and it worked! At the time, I was reading the book *E Squared*[39].

127. Write yourself a cheque

The idea here is to write yourself a cheque with the amount of money you'd like to manifest and a date for when you'd like the money to come into your life. You can then place the cheque somewhere where you can see it on a daily basis. When you look at it, feel good as if the cheque really is real.

45

It sounds ridiculous, but you could try this out for 30 days. I once tried it out for a small amount of money and actually received the amount that was on the cheque which was nice as I wasn't earning much at the time.

128. Be grateful for everything you have
Write a gratitude journal or before you go to bed, think of the best thing that happened to you that day and feel grateful.

Stuff to give up
30 day challenges

129. Sending unfriendly emails
I went through a phase where I thought I was being efficient by sending really short emails to people. For example, if someone had asked me to do something, when I'd done it, I'd email back with, 'Done'. It was only when I received a few of these short and to the point emails myself that I realised how rude I was being.

130. Offloading onto others
If you're a consistent complainer, can you find another outlet? Fair enough if you have problems you need to discuss, but if it's one thing after the other, are you or the other person actually benefitting from it? Perhaps write your thoughts down then throw them away, do something creative or try meditating.

131. Giving people your advice when it's

unasked for

We might think we're being helpful with this one, but often we're not. We often give advice based on our own experiences or limited knowledge of something.

132. Being a people pleaser

It's nice to be there for others, but at what expense? Don't neglect your own interests or resentments might build.

133. Waiting around for the 'right' time

If you're a perfectionist, this one's for you. Unless there really is a 'right time', ask yourself what you can do right now to make a start of something.

134. Comparing yourself obsessively to others

Sometimes this can drive you into action, but at other times it can either add to your ego, make you feel insecure or stop you from developing connections with people.

135. Your grudges

For this one, I did certain heart practice meditations. I also think it's good to remember that when you do hold a grudge, it's only yourself that you're hurting, as cliched as that sounds. This quote by Buddha explains it better than me: *"Holding on to anger is like grasping a hot coal with the intent of throwing it at someone else; you are the one who gets burned."*

136. Watching TV

If you never seem to have time for things, but spend a significant time watching TV, consider switching the TV for something else — at least for 30 days. Or, to ease in slowly, limit yourself to a certain number of hours a week.

137. Your phone

This one is from my friend Lily, and my first reaction to this was, 'Is it possible in today's society?' I did do this for 10 days during my silent Vipassana meditation[40] retreat, and it was one of the most refreshing things I've done, so I recommend it. If 30 days is too much, put a time limit on the amount of time you spend on your phone instead.

138. Resisting stuff

I'll quote Carl Jung for this one. "What you resist persists." So, if there is anything in your life you've been ignoring, now is the time to face it. Learn to accept what you can't change and change what you can. This one is really about self acceptance and not judging yourself or creating resistance to any of your emotions or feelings.

139. Blaming everyone and everything

This includes yourself. Hopefully you don't have things to blame every day, but if you do find yourself complaining a lot, see what happens when you let things go for a month. Allow yourself to feel whatever it is you need to feel in the moment, but if you allow little things to affect you for the rest of the day, week, month or even year, you're only hurting yourself.

140. Being horrible to yourself

This includes negative self talk, not giving yourself any time out, and not taking good care of yourself.

141. Something you've been wanting to give up for a long time

I'm not advocating that you give up a long-time addiction in 30 days as studies show that the average time for breaking bad habits takes approximately 66 days[41]. This, of course will vary from person to person and it depends what you're giving up. However, you could make a start in 30 days — seek out people who could help you or read a book that's been recommended to you, based on what it is you want to give up.

Themed mood
30 day challenges

142. Try a themed mood challenge

These are a bit different. Rather than doing any one thing every day, you've basically got a theme for your life for 30 days. Far too often we tell ourselves, I'm a person who is unproductive, lazy, uncreative... With these challenges, all you have to do is set the intention at the start of your 30 days to be as productive, creative, confident, generous (insert theme here) as you like and see how your behaviour changes. If you have a theme, you might find yourself being more attracted to people, resources and opportunities related to that theme.

Meditation and inner life
30 day challenges

143. Try the OSHO Nataraj Meditation[42]

This one focuses on dance, and doesn't involve you being a stereotypically good dancer. It's more about losing yourself in the meditation of movement. I've only tried this once but it was one of the most exhilarating and freeing meditations I've done.

144. Try the eye wandering exercise

Spend just a few minutes each day allowing your eyes to wander from object to object around you. The idea is to let your eyes move without labeling or judging anything.

145. Make your hobby your meditation

Yoga and meditation are practices in awareness. If seated meditation isn't for you, why not practise being more aware in an existing hobby or sport you love doing such as making art, running or playing an instrument.

146. Spend five minutes focusing on your breath

You can be anywhere for this one — on the train, in a queue or at work. It might not seem like you're doing much, but investing as little as five minutes a day to take some time out and focus on your breath could help to give you more energy, reduce stress and help you to focus more.

147. Practise alternate nostril breathing to feel more balanced

To practise, alternate nostril breathing, gently close your right nostril with your right thumb and inhale through the left nostril. Using your ring and little fingers, close off the left nostril and exhale through the right nostril. Continue to repeat this process for up to five minutes. For specific instructions, read the Hatha Yoga Pradipika[43].

148. Try body scan meditations

You can practise this whilst lying down or sitting with your back in a neutral position. With your eyes closed, gently take your awareness to different parts of your body, moving from the feet up to the head and from the head back down to the feet.

149. Music meditation

If you find seated quiet meditation a struggle to do regularly, perhaps start with music. Select a few tracks you love and spend time meditating to them — absorbing yourself fully in what you're listening to.

150. Try different chakra meditations

There are lots of different guided chakra meditations out there, but one of my favourites is an 11 minute track called Bija Mantras by musician Russil Paul[44]. As you're listening to the sounds, move your awareness to the different chakras. Whether you believe in chakras or not, I find these sounds really beautiful to listen to.

151. Dance like noone is watching

I took part in a Shakti dance[45] workshop once at Glastonbury Festival which involved dancing to music in any way you liked. Dancing can be such a powerful meditative and transformative experience if you can lose your inhibitions. For this one, start by selecting different kinds of music to play, and move your body to the music in any way that feels right. Don't worry about how you look.

152. Incorporate the four paths of yoga into your life

You can practise yoga asanas purely to help you relax or get fit. However, I think it's equally as important to become aware that the physical side of yoga (i.e the yoga postures) are just one small part. The four paths of yoga which I originally learnt about through practising Sivananda Yoga[46], are as follows:

- Jnana yoga — the yoga of wisdom, knowledge and contemplation

- Bhakti yoga — the yoga of love and devotion
- Karma yoga — the yoga of selfless service
- Raja yoga — the yoga of meditation, which also includes hatha yoga

153. Live by the 8 Limbs of Yoga

As well as the four paths of yoga, The Eight Limbs of Yoga were created by Patanjali and are part of Raja Yoga. For 30 days, if you're used to practising mainly yoga asanas, familiarise yourself with the other limbs of yoga and put them into practise too. Start by reading The Yoga Sutras of Patanjali[47].

154. Practise body tapping techniques to prepare you for meditation

Gently tapping different parts of your body from the head down to your toes for five to ten minutes can be an incredibly powerful way to help you relax and relieve stress before sitting still in meditation. This was one of the exercises introduced to me on my meditation teacher training. You might also want to look into the Emotional Freedom Technique[48].

155. Get the Headspace App[49] if you're new to meditation

If you've never tried any meditation before, the Headspace App is a brilliant place to start and is free to use for 10 days, but the techniques are enough to keep you going for much longer. There are plenty of meditation apps out there, but I only have first hand experience with Headspace.

156. Practise heart based meditation practices to let go of emotional baggage

Although there are hundreds of different heart based meditation practices, the first one I ever tried was called

Open Heart Meditation at the Lotus Centre[50] in Hobart, Tasmania. It was a beautiful practice focusing on forgiveness, opening the heart and letting go of emotional baggage. You can also access the same meditation I did in Hobart online if you search for *Open Heart Meditation*.

157. Practise Buddhist Loving and Kindness meditations

As the name suggests, Buddhist Loving and Kindness meditations[51] help to increase compassion, empathy and help you to learn to forgive yourself and others.

158. Practise the Brahmari or the humming bee breath exercise

Find a comfortable place to sit and keep your eyes open or closed for this exercise. Start by taking a few breaths at your own pace. Then inhale through your nose whilst keeping your mouth closed. On your exhale, make a gently humming sound and repeat the process for a few more rounds. This exercise is known in yoga as a pranayama exercise that helps to relieve stress and anxiety. For more detailed instructions, start by reading the Hatha Yoga Pradipika[52].

159. Practise the imagination wandering exercise

This is something I like to practise every now and again. It started as an exercise from the book *Feel the fear and do it anyway*[53]. I start by imagining myself in a wide open field or meadow. I then allow my mind to wander. Where do you go? Who are you with? What do you do? I often do this to help give me clarity as to where I am in my life at any given point. It only really works if you're a visual person, and it's not for everyone.

160. Practise Kapalbhati breathing to make

your head glow

This pranayama exercise is also known as the shining skull exercise as it is said to make the practitioner glow, according to the Hatha Yoga Pradipika. It could also help to give you more energy and improve circulation. It's best to practise this one from a teacher first to make sure you're doing it right. If you take a Sivananda[54] Yoga class, it is one of the pranayama exercises practised at the start.

161. Practise Breath of Fire

This one looks similar to kapalbhati but the inhalation and exhalation are equal. Go to a yoga class where you can learn this one first hand from a teacher to make sure you're doing it right and then try practising it for 30 days. For me, this feels really good when I practise it first thing in the morning as it's so energising. You can read about more of the benefits on kundalini Yoga Info[55].

162. Go on a local pilgrimage

There's no reason why you couldn't plan a local 30 day pilgrimage near to where you live. You don't need to leave your home for 30 days or fly to another country — instead, research spiritual places of significance where you live and visit them instead or go to places that have a personal meaning to you. You could also incorporate silent morning walks into your local pilgrimage and get others involved.

163. Practise mantra meditation

The only mantra I have experience with over an extended period of time is OM, which can be incredibly therapeutic to repeat silently before meditation. Some people believe certain mantras can lead to specific experiences. Others believe that mantras are simply a tool to help still the mind and it doesn't matter what you repeat. I'll leave you to make your own mind up through your own experiences.

164. Meditate with singing bowls

I love the sound of my singing bowl and so do cats for some reason — which I take to be a good sign. You can either use your singing bowl as a type of object meditation, play it for a few minutes before your regular meditation or make a recording of it which you can listen to whilst you meditate.

165. Meditate at 4am

Although you can meditate at any time of the day, I've often loved meditating at 4am because there's such a magical stillness in the air and waking up at this time makes you feel like you've got a head start on the world.

166. Practise meditating in your dreams

If you're a regular lucid dreamer, according to Andrew Holocek from the course Dream Sculpting[56], when you meditate in a lucid dream it's supposed to be more effective than when you do it in waking life.

167. Practise everyday mindfulness

For this one, you don't need to change anything you physically do. You just need to become more present and aware of your everyday actions. This could include, slowing down your eating to really taste and appreciate the food, listening to the sounds around you, or slowing down your walking to see how your perception of the world changes. You could start with just five minutes a day.

168. Try object meditation

This is about choosing an object or something external to focus on. It could be the flame of a candle, bright stars on a dark sky or a mandala — to name just a few things.

169. Try meditating with prayer beads

You can use these to help calm the mind while you meditate,

or in conjunction with a mantra. Although I don't personally use prayer or mala beads to meditate, many people do, such as my Mum, and find them really helpful.

170. Try 5Rhythms[57]
For me 5Rhythms was an incredibly uplifting and energising form of meditation through dance. If you enjoy movement practices and you can find a class or workshop near to where you live, I highly recommend it. There's no reason why you can't then continue to dance at home, although, this is a practice which can be just as much about connecting with others as it is about yourself.

171. Reflect on the question who am I?
The Indian Sage Sri Ramana Maharshi[58] is an advocate of asking this one question — Who am I? — when you're on an inward journey. Rather than literally asking the question every day, meditate on it and believe that you will get the answers that are right for you.

172. Practise yoga nidra
Yoga nidra is possibly one of the most relaxing and insightful meditation techniques I've done. There are hundreds of guided yoga nidra sessions online, but I recommend any by Richard Miller[59].

173. Spend each day being as 'present' as possible and absorbed in everything you do
Make the most of simple acts and routine tasks. Life will feel brighter and you will hopefully feel more fulfilled. It's not often what we've got or where we are, but our attitude to what life throws our way.

Recreation, art and creative 30 day challenges

Art practical (drawing, painting and sculpture)
Writing
Photography, music and media art
Upcycling, crafts and textiles
Recreation and fun

Art practical (drawing, painting, and sculpture) 30 day challenges

174. Draw a postcard sized picture every day

Collect 30 postcard sized bits of paper, select a theme to draw and create a miniature piece of art every day. By the end of a month, you can display all the postcards together and possibly frame it for your home or give it away as a present. Experiment with different coloured squares, inks, pens and other drawing tools. And remember, not to be too perfectionist about it.

175. Learn to draw faces

You don't necessarily need to enrol on a drawing course, unless you want the social aspect. There are many online portrait drawing tutorials that you can follow for free. Get yourself a sketchbook and be amazed at the progress you will make.

176. Learn to draw in sight-size

This is an ancient technique that involves drawing something in front of you precisely and accurately so your subject matter appears to be the same size as what you're drawing on your paper or canvas. It might take you longer than a month to master this, but you'll learn a lot in 30 days. Rather than spending each day on a new drawing, spend the whole month on one small piece. I've seen people who are completely new to drawing produce excellent results when they apply sight-size techniques.

177. Draw with your eyes closed

If you're new to drawing, this can be quite a fun exercise to get you used to making marks on paper without really caring about the outcome. You could spend 30 days drawing purely with your eyes closed, or combine this with another 30 day drawing challenge.

178. Draw with your opposite hand

Similar to drawing with your eyes closed, this gets you used to making interesting expressive marks on the page and it gets you to stop worrying so much about what you're producing. I've created some interesting life drawings with my left hand.

179. Learn to sculpt with clay

Get some cheap clay or source some yourself, decide on what you'd like to sculpt and give yourself 30 days to make it, which would include finding someone to fire it for you and glaze it.

180. Draw something upside down

If you want to draw something representationally from a photograph, it's often easier to turn it upside down because it forces you to look at the shapes and tones of the picture rather than drawing what you think the objects should look like. Spend one month on one piece or experiment with smaller upside down sketches every day.

181. Draw on scrap bits of paper

You don't necessarily need the best water colour paper or expensive sketchbooks to produce art. You can draw on almost anything — old newspapers, receipts, sheet music, old books. I recently started making yoga related artwork in the pages of an old dictionary.

182. Make rubbings of interesting surfaces and textures

I recently went to Morocco on holiday and wished I'd carried a thick pencil and a sketchbook around with me to make rubbings of all the beautiful surfaces and geometric shapes. I'm sure wherever you are in the world, you can find one interesting pattern to make a rubbing of every day. You could then add all the rubbings together to frame or use the patterns to influence further pieces of art.

183. Make a sculpture from random objects

Collect drawing pins, old toys from Christmas crackers and other seemingly random bits of junk you no longer need. Make something abstract or more specific, or just enjoy the process of making something.

184. Learn how to draw sacred geometry

Drawing sacred geometry isn't as hard as it looks. Get yourself some paper, a pencil and a compass and you're onto a great start. If you have Adobe Illustrator or Photoshop, there are really good tutorials online for drawing sacred geometry patterns on a computer.

185. Learn to carve things from wood

It took me a whole day once to carve a simple wooden spoon from a small tree branch. You'd be surprised how much you can make out of fallen branches, some creative vision and a knife. Spending as little as 20 minutes a day, you could have something beautifully carved at the end of the month.

186. Draw using a Spirograph

I loved my Spirograph as a child and I still love using Spirograph as an adult. Enjoy the process of making Spirograph art or incorporate Spirograph patterns in existing artworks.

187. Creature a miniature 'junk art' sculpture

Gather together cereal boxes, old scraps of fabrics, jars, bottles, old computer keyboards, cutlery you no longer need...and make a miniature world, or choose a random object or animal such as a car or dinosaur and see if you can make a miniature version of it using scrap materials.

188. Try free drawing

This is how children draw to some extent — freely and without caring what other people think. Free drawing allows you to doodle, draw and make marks on a surface without worrying about the outcome of the piece. You're drawing straight from your imagination with this one and in some respects, it could be a form of art therapy. The key is to not care about the outcome and just enjoy the act of expressing yourself.

189. Make a 30 page hand drawn comic book

Team up with writer and create a comic book together in 30 days. If you learn bookbinding which is easier than you might think, you can make the whole book yourself.

190. Doodle

Doodling can be really therapeutic and a really good way to relieve stress. Doodle on scrap bits of paper, a notebook you can use while you're on the go, or 30 pieces of paper you can collage together at the end of your challenge.

191. Create a painting in a month

If you never know when to stop a painting, giving yourself a time limit might help. Alternatively, if you tend to rush things, giving yourself 30 hours over a month might help.

192. Paint a canvas in one colour

You could buy or make yourself 30 small canvases, then paint each one a different colour for a month. You don't have to use flat colour. Take inspiration from artists like Mark Rothko[60] and Howard Hodgkin[61]. You could use all the colours or stick to a colour theme if you wanted to display all your canvases together in your home as one piece. This surely has to beat buying coloured canvases for your house.

193. Paint a mural

In our house growing up, we painted a mural on the garden wall which looked pretty good as ivy used to grow around it. Once you've got your design, sketch it out and get your whole family involved.

194. Make land art

Take inspiration from Andy Goldsworthy[62] and create beautiful temporary land art made from the natural environment. Leaves, stones, bark and stray pieces of wood can be your starting point and the rest is up to you. Photograph each piece as you go along.

195. Try action painting

You might be familiar with Jackson Pollock's[63] paintings, which can also be called action paintings as he used to pretty much dance with the paint as he was creating his art. The idea here is to enjoy the process. This is essentially what the Abstract Expressionist art movement was all about. You don't even need to use huge surfaces — just make sure you put down plenty of newspaper if you're doing it in your house, or you're giving it to your kids as an activity to do.

196. Collect paint sample strips and make

art with them

For a while I collected about 100 colourful paint sample strips and then used printing ink to print on top of them. The sample strips I used had names like cherry cheesecake, seal or nude. I then printed the picture on each one. Alternatively, if they don't have names, use the coloured strips to cut up, collage together and make bold patterns with them which could then be framed and displayed in your home.

197. Spend 20 minutes working on a piece of mandala artwork

You can meditate with mandalas once they're done. Or drawing and colouring them in is an incredibly therapeutic exercise. I loved making mandalas as a 30 day challenge, which then inspired me to set up my Etsy shop.

198. Spend 15 minutes colouring every day

Get yourself a colouring book or draw out your own designs to colour in with felt tip pens or sharpies. There's something so satisfying about applying bright bold colours to paper.

199. Make dictionary art

Look up your hobbies and make art on that page related to the word. I created a Namaste mandala in my dictionary. If they're good, you could make copies, frame them and maybe sell them as prints.

200. Design tattoos

You could sketch out tattoo ideas or learn to draw henna tattoos. Who knows, it could be the start of a new career.

Writing 30 day challenges

201. Write a book in 30 days

It doesn't matter if you're a professional writer or complete beginner, you could use the website National Novel Writing Month (Nanowrimo)[64] to help you to write a book in a month with the help of all the online resources and community. It's also free to use. Alternatively, set your own agenda. The first draft of this book was written in 30 days.

202. Write a blog post a day

I did this for several months and discovered that I wasn't always producing decent articles. This, however, is a good one to build your self discipline. It'll be easier if you start with a list of article titles. You don't always have to publish each article. This is more about getting into the habit of writing every day.

203. Write a themed poem a day

You could put random words in a hat and select two words every day to write a new poem from — similar to the poet from the film *Before Sunrise*.

204. Write a series of personalised A-Z guides

This could work in a similar way to a diary, but might be less cringey to look back on in years to come. Theme your guides with categories such as A-Z of my favourite films, things I love, favourite songs...You get the idea.

205. Keep an 'everyday' travel journal

We keep travel journals when we've visited faraway exotic places, but isn't the whole of life a journey. Sorry to get all cliched on you. Take photos, collect travel tickets, draw, write...doing this might help you notice things that you previously took for granted about your everyday life.

206. Write a poem by selecting words from the dictionary at random

This was an exercise from a creative writing workshop I attended at university. You could limit yourself to two words a day or see if you can write a whole poem a day using over 10 random words. Your only rules are — use words at random from a dictionary.

207. Write a song

If you're already a songwriter or musician, this one is for you. You might not necessarily produce the best songs, but it might help to spark ideas.

208. Create your own cookbook in a month or food blog

If you love experimenting in the kitchen, write down all your recipes, whilst taking photos of the whole process. At the end of the month, all you have to do is arrange it all and get it made into a book. You could also do this if you have lots of yummy family recipes that have been passed down through the generations — providing they're not secrets.

209. Be a journalist

If you want to write good journalistic pieces, don't necessarily wait for someone to choose you. Figure out what you're passionate about, go out there, do research and write about it.

210. Keep an ideas book for 30 days

It doesn't matter what area of work you're in for this one — if you're someone with lots of ideas, you might write down a really good one during your 30 days. Use Evernote or just keep a small notebook with you at all times.

211. Take a notebook with you everywhere

If you're into writing, this goes without saying. Make observations of people, write down things that make you laugh, describe your surroundings, try freewriting...just record something every day and see what new ideas and inspiration occurs as a result.

212. Write down things that made you laugh

You can look back on it when you're sad to help cheer you up or read it to someone who's sad.

213. Try free writing

Who knows what new ideas might occur when you do this — either that or you'll be left with a page of incomprehensible scrawl. All you need to do is set a timer, grab a pen and paper and write whatever comes out of your pen. You're not allowed to stop and think or worry about spelling and grammar. After 30 days, reread what you've written and see if it sparks any new ideas.

214. Learn calligraphy

Everyone will admire your handwriting when you send them cards, and if you get really good, you could start making online tutorials or hold calligraphy workshops.

215. Make a quote jar

Find a jar that you can fit your hand into and every day for a month, write out an inspiring quote that makes you feel good. You can then put the quotes into the jar, so people can pull them out when they come over.

Photography, music and media art 30 day challenges

216. Take a photo a day on your way to work

If you can find one beautiful thing to photograph on your trip to work, it might make commuting a little more interesting. If you need inspiration, looking up might help — sometimes there are intricate details in the tops of old buildings or maybe the sky is particularly pretty.

217. Teach yourself Photoshop, InDesign and Illustrator

You can pick up the basics pretty quickly for any of these programs in a two day course, so you could absolutely learn the basics in a month using free online tutorials.

218. Teach yourself photography

We live in a world where photography has been reduced to pointing and clicking. I'm certainly not complaining about this, but it does mean that we might be inclined to learn less about this art form. Most digital cameras have manual settings. You can then learn about ISO, shutter speed and composition online, from books or workshops.

219. Sell a photograph a day

If you're into your photography, try selling one photograph a day online, or create some prints of your work to sell at a high end market or pop up shop.

220. Photograph one beautiful thing every

day

By the end of the month, you should hopefully have a lovely collection you might even want to print out and put up in your home. Doing this will also hopefully allow you to view your everyday world with fresh eyes. Sometimes, when you get into a routine, you stop noticing what's right in front of you. View the world through a photographer's eye and learn to see beauty that's all around.

221. Choose a photography theme

Photograph the sky, the colour green or the same tree under different shades of light. Rather than aiming for perfection every day, enjoy the process of taking photos and see what new ideas and inspiration come out of it.

222. Teach yourself to play a new instrument

If you're like me, you might already have an instrument lying around which you haven't got around to learning properly yet. After owning a wooden flute for a year without knowing how to play it, I taught myself a few songs and scales as a 30 day challenge. All you have to do is find a local teacher, watch online tutorials or pick up a book. You could also ask someone who already plays that instrument what the best thing to focus on would be for a month.

223. Make a musical instrument

I once met a flute boxer — that's someone who beatboxes using a flute. It sounded incredible and he'd made his instrument himself. You don't have to make something as complicated as this though — loads of people invent really strange instruments from random junk or even old furniture. For inspiration, have a look at the work by multimedia artist Thomas Truax[65].

324. Learn how to read music

You might not get to pro standards in 30 days, but you can tackle the basics. And if you're already a musician who can't read music, see how learning to read music might influence your playing. It might be no help at all, but you could give it a go.

325. Learn to play music through feeling and intuition

My friend Fiona who is a really talented musician gave a me a flute lesson that was all about using your intuition and feeling to learn music. It was one of the best music lessons I've had and completely different to the approach I was taught when I was at school and playing the oboe not very well.

226. Sing

Teach yourself a new song, practise scales and do singing exercises every day. See if you can skill swap with someone and learn how to sing firsthand from a teacher.

227. Make a documentary or video

There's a documentary film I love called *Dark Days* which was shot on a cheap camera with pretty much no budget for the project. It ended up winning awards and today is still recognised as one of the best Indie documentaries. So, if money or lack of equipment is stopping you, this film is living proof that you could produce something amazing using what you have right now.

228. Create an online course

If you've got skills you could share, start an online course which you could sell or offer for free. If you did sell it, you could get affiliate marketers to help you out by offering them a percentage of the money. Use your own website or one of the many other platforms out there such as Udemy.

229. Teach yourself video editing
Learn a new technique a day, practise editing clips together using footage from your phone and watch some online tutorials.

230. Record your own guided meditations
If you're into meditation or stress management and you've got the voice for it, this is one for you. You could start by writing some yoga nidra scripts.

231. Film the progress of your 30 day challenge
I'd be curious to watch someone's 30 day challenge. It could also be a good motivator to keep going.

Upcycling, crafts and textiles 30 day challenges

232. Make an item of clothing
Start with a simple pattern and take it from there. You'll probably be better off with a sewing machine for this one, but it's still possible by hand — just select some interesting fabrics and sewing threads, which you will be able to pick up pretty cheaply from charity shops.

233. Make sculptures from old hardback books

I've got a beautiful hardback book that's been carved into the letter 'C' which was a birthday present from a friend. I'm sure you could make your own sculptures if you picked up some old books you like the look of from a charity shop and gather some necessary tools together.

234. Collect travel tickets and make a collage

Be inspired by the artist Kurt Schwitters[66] who used old tickets and other scraps of paper to make beautiful collages with.

235. Draw on maps and frame them

I think maps look really cool in general, especially old antique ones. You could find maps of your hometown, frame them as they are, do simple line drawings on them, or even write out some of your memories of being in certain places.

236. Make a patchwork throw with 30 squares

I was given some beautiful silk offcuts of sari fabric from my Mum and thought they'd make a beautiful shawl or throw. You could use scrap pieces of materials from old clothes or go to a fabric shop and gather together some offcuts from there.

237. Knit a scarf doing a few lines a day

This used to be my go-to Christmas present. Aside from making something functional, I love knitting and find the whole process really relaxing. I've actually got a really long scarf, that's completely impractical — I started knitting it about eight years ago. It's big enough to wrap around a small house.

238. Create a textile wall hanging

Rather than using paper to make art for your walls, use fabric as your base. You could draw, sew, weave or paint straight onto the surface then find an appropriate way to hang it in your home or give it away as a present. You might want to also consider learning how to do textile batiks or silk paintings. However, you'd probably have to attend workshops or classes for these to do them properly.

239. Make a weaving from found tree branches

When my parents moved to the countryside, my Mum started making loads of beautiful weavings from small tree branches, bits of wool, string, dried flowers and off-cuts of fabric. They look really good with fairy lights or with lamps behind them and they cost no money to make.

240. Customise old clothes

Even just dyeing discoloured clothes can make a huge difference. But if you want to get more creative, gather together buttons, ribbons, beads, fabric pens and explore. See if you can create something beautiful (or at least wearable again) from at least three things you no longer wear in your wardrobe. Or you could just swap clothes with friends to customise.

241. Make a scrap fabric rug

I think these look stunning. In 30 days, you could make a small rug for the side of your bed. All you need to do is gather together some fabric, pick a braiding technique, find some how-to manuals and get going.

242. Make paper stencil lanterns

I went to a workshop at *Eastern Curve Garden* in London, where we made stencils using black paper, which were then stuck to the inside of glass jars. With tea light candles inside they looked so beautiful. I've also used the same technique with paper lampshades. You can then drape fairy lights inside them. Just check before, that you're not creating any fire hazards and that the lights or candles you're using are safe.

243. Make cushion covers

Give all your home cushions a makeover or spend a month making one large complicated cushion cover embellished with beads, buttons and fancy stitchwork.

244. Make jewellery

You can get cheap jewellery starter kits online as well as reusing broken pieces of jewellery, plus any buttons, beads or knickknacks you already own. You could challenge yourself to make a piece a day, or spend a month making something really special.

245. Learn bookbinding

This isn't as hard as you might think. I did a bookbinding workshop whilst at university and learnt how to do it in a few hours. All you need is some paper to bind, PVA glue, thin thread, a small hand hacksaw and a pencil. I've made several small notebooks using scrap paper and when they're done properly, they can look really professional.

246. Make bleach paint t-shirts

I don't have any first-hand experience with this one, but I think they look beautiful. It might take some time to learn how to do this properly, but you can certainly make a start in 30 days. Next step — find some credible instructions online, stay safe when working with bleach and start making some unique one off bleach t-shirts.

247. Upcycle your scrabble letters

Make a personalised piece of scrabble art, super glue letters to rings or cufflinks, or make coasters.

248. Collect together 20 random objects. What can you make in a month?

This is more an exercise in lateral thinking, but you might also end up creating something really useful or pretty for your home.

249. Make handbags, purses and laptop cases from old hardback books

I have a laptop case made from an old hardback encyclopedia which has my date of birth on the spine — 1986. It was cleverly made by my friend Kiran who added a zip to the opening. I'm sure you could do the same thing with smaller books to make purses and wallets.

250. Knit a plastic bag shopping bag

If you do this, make sure you don't use biodegradable plastic bags like I did. In a year's time, the whole bag disintegrated into plastic dust. However, I'd knitted a pretty sturdy shopping bag while it lasted. You can probably find some decent instructions online, but all you need to do is cut plastic bags into long strips. I then tied the strips together and started knitting.

251. Paint patterns on old shoes and bags

I've never actually worn shoes I've painted patterns on as they've always clashed with everything, but I once painted a bag with nail varnish, which I then wore to a wedding.

252. Make a board game

You could choose an existing board game like chess and make your own board and pieces, or you could get inventive and make up a whole new game using craft supplies from around your house and old cereal boxes. You could make it personalised for your family.

253. Upcycle furniture with newspaper, magazines, sheet music and comics

Think twice before throwing out ugly furniture. You could cover it with sheet music or other interesting images and either keep it or sell it.

254. Make a mosaic table top or frame

What I love about mosaics is that they often look really impressive, whether they're part of pattern or not, and they're really accessible to make. You can either pick up mosaic squares for this or use old tiles and plates.

255. Do up an old bike

My Dad went through a phase of buying old broken bikes from eBay to do up. If you know what you're doing I can imagine this would be a really fun project. Alternatively, if you know nothing about fixing bikes, you could at least spray paint it, which is what I did with one of my old bikes.

256. Decorate stones

I remember making ladybird stones as a child which looked good in the garden. You could paint mandalas on them or paint them to match the colours in your home and put them around candles.

257. Make a piece of furniture

Take inspiration from *Pinterest*, find a how-to guide and make a piece of furniture for your home in 30 days.

Recreation and fun
30 day challenges

258. Play more
When was the last time you really indulged in play? For this one it could be anything from taking 10 minutes out of your day to do something spontaneous, dance, do something you love or wouldn't normally do...either alone or with others. This one is for you if you want to be less serious, you can't remember the last time you laughed really hard, or you have no idea what to do when you read the word play.

259. Create a bucket list of 30 things in 30 days
If you want to go one step further, you could also create a Pinterest board to go with each item on your list. Having something visual to look at might make it happen faster.

260. Create or work on your blog
Write, research, take photos, learn how to edit and upload videos...Do a little bit every day and see where it takes you.

261. Watch documentaries
You could try switching your regular TV programmes for documentaries, or try to find documentaries on subjects you know nothing about. I'm a bit obsessed with documentaries on space.

262. Become a master of magic
It probably takes a lot longer than a month, but you could pick one trick to master really well over the course of a month. I've only ever met about two people in my life who

could do some really cool magic tricks that I still don't know how they did it.

263. Switch your daily newspaper for a specialist magazine

Subscribe to a hobby magazine instead, or pick up a new magazine to read every week and read it on your commute to work instead of the free newspaper.

264. Make yourself and other people laugh

Start with yourself and then aim to make at least one person laugh every day —because we all need more laughter in our lives.

265. Play one good song a day first thing in the morning

Change your alarm to your favourite song and let good music be the first thing you hear. Recommended for cold winter months when waking up might be harder.

266. Make your own beer, wine or sloe gin

This one is for those who can legally drink and if you do decide to do this one, always remember to drink responsibly. If what you make is good enough, you could give them to people as presents.

267. Look at the stars

This is how I spent my last New Year's Eve — on a roof in the Atlas Mountains gazing up at such an incredible starry sky. If you're lucky enough to live in a place where you can see the night sky clearly, don't take it for granted. Star gazing is one of the best meditations you can do. You could also learn some constellations at the same time.

268. Press flowers

You can press flowers pretty easily in a hardback book then use them to make so many different things from decorative flower collages, coasters, lanterns, candle holders...

269. Learn numerology
I'm not sure whether I believe in this or not, but I still like reading about what certain numbers in my life mean.

270. Get an allotment or grow veg in your garden
We all know freshly grown veg tastes so much better than the stuff in supermarkets. Seek out your local allotment or start a veg patch in your garden. Make creative use of small spaces with window boxes and old pallets which could be used to grow things up the wall. Or you could start by growing a few tomato plants inside.

271. Make a family tree
Start looking into it online and see what you find out. It could also be given as a present to other people in your family.

272. Learn graphology
This is the study of handwriting and what it says about you. I have a book about it on my bookshelf and it's surprisingly fascinating. If you start this one though, you won't be able to stop looking at the way people write and trying to work out what they're all about.

273. Build a luxury permanent den in your garden
If you've got the space, why not? You could use it to meditate in, play music whilst pretending you're living in the wilderness or it could become an alternative work space. Be creative and use discarded pieces of wood and fallen tree

branches.

274. Learn henna tattooing

Henna tattoos can look so beautiful. Spend a bit of time each day mastering this art. Maybe you could start giving people henna tattoos in the summer.

275. See how far you can get hitchhiking

This one is for those who are over 18 only. At the time, I didn't call it a 30 day challenge, but 10 years ago, I did spend a month hitchhiking with a few friends from northern Finland to the Netherlands. If you do this, remember always to stay safe, go with someone else and always trust your intuition. Read about how to stay safe hitchhiking first. This article *Hitchhiker's Safety*[67] might be a good place to start.

276. Design a treasure hunt

In a month you've got the time to design a really elaborate one, perhaps for a special occasion for someone you care about.

277. Read a different newspaper

If you usually read the same newspaper or news site, switch it to a completely different one and see what you learn and what you hate/love about it.

278. Listen to a new podcast a day

There's a saying that you are the average of the five people you spend the most time with. If you're not entirely happy with your five, listen to the podcasts of some people you admire.

279. Learn origami

I walked into one of the lecturer's offices at the university where I used to work and it was filled with origami creations

— really elaborate ones. I didn't ask her when she had time for all of it, but I definitely admired her creativity. In a month, you could probably produce something quite spectacular if you learn one new origami creation a day.

280. Laminate

Laminate pressed flowers, images you like from magazines, drawings...and make your creations into jewellery, keyrings, or mobiles.

281. Plant a flower a day — in your garden or just in random places

Packets of seeds barely cost a thing. Plant the seeds to create a really spectacular garden or start a veg patch.

282. Start bird watching

You could start by installing a bird feeder in your garden, then record how many birds you see in your garden each day.

283. Create themed playlists

I've always admired people who can play the perfect music for each occasion. Creating playlists is a fine art, but when you get it right, you'll save loads of time trawling through music trying to find the right song. Examples could be Nostalgia from the 90's, Music that makes you want to dance, early morning yoga music holiday car music memories...

284. Watch the sunrise

Team this one with an early morning meditation and you'll feel really refreshed to start the day.

285. Write out random directions to see where you end up

You could spend 10 minutes doing this each day and take photographs of where you end up. You could even accompany your directions with some rules such as smile at the first person you see when you turn right, or leave a nice note for a stranger to pick up.

286. Live like a tourist in your home city

I still haven't been to some of the major tourist spots in London and I know I'm not alone with this one. You don't necessarily have to seek out all the well know attractions — this one is about seeing your hometown or city with new eyes.

287. Go foraging

Set out with a plan and connect with the land. Gathering sloe berries for sloe gin is a good one in the autumn.

288. Teach your dog new tricks

Whenever I go back to my parents, I love teaching my parents collie dog Meg new tricks, which she then often forgets when I leave. There's only so much you can do in a few days, but she did manage to jump through a hoop after one visit. With consistent teaching over 30 days think of the progress you could make!

289. Walk slowly in busy places

Even if it's for just five minutes a day, walk really slowly and treat it as your daily meditation. Clear your head and focus only on what's around you and see how your perception changes and what new things you notice. If you're not a fan of seated meditations, you might really enjoy this one.

290. Play with Lego

Look at some of Nathan Sawaya's amazing Lego artwork[68] and feel inspired. If you don't already have Lego, you can pick up assorted Lego brick bags online pretty cheaply.

291. Listen to songs from your youth

Think about the best year of your life, and listen to all the songs from that year or time period — maybe picking a song a day, to see if it lifts your spirits.

292. Visit local tourist destinations in your area and do what's opposite

This one was my cousin John's idea. Visit local tourist destinations or popular places of interest, turn your back on it and engage yourself in whatever is in front of you. It could lead to some interesting conversations or happenings.

Home life, professional life and finance
30 day challenges

Home life
Productivity at work
Career boosting and work
Money and finance

Home life 30 day challenges

293. Give your home a complete spring clean

My Mum always used to tell people that she'd give the house a really thorough clean once a year and they'd look horrified thinking she only cleaned once a year. What she meant was that she went through each room clearing out clutter and throwing unwanted stuff away. When you break this lengthy task down, it's totally do-able in a month, providing you don't live in a castle.

294. Start an upcycling project for your home

After your spring clean, you could start redecorating on a budget. I've written out loads of specific suggestions for **upcycling projects** in the recreation and creativity chapter so I won't go into detail here.

295. Leave nice surprise notes in your home

My boyfriend sometimes leaves me notes and I really love it. A friend also once left a nice note for my next door neighbours to say how much she liked their piano music. It might seem like a small thing, but the person receiving the note will appreciate the gesture.

296. Install a blackboard for messages

Similar to the notes, use a blackboard to write messages to make people laugh, or quotes, affirmations…where everyone can see it.

297. Pay attention when doing everyday

tasks

I struggle with this one. When I've done something again and again and again, It's easy to just go onto autopilot. But, when you're in a routine, isn't this a lot of your life? See how differently you feel when you make a conscious effort to really focus on what you're doing.

298. Fix broken stuff in your home

Make a note of what needs fixing and make plans over 30 days to fix everything. If you're not used to doing this stuff, can you learn? If not, can you swap skills with someone, or get it fixed professionally?

299. Live with limited material items

There's been times in my life when most of my stuff could fit into a backpack. I'm not suggesting you throw out anything, but you could try limiting what you use for a month to see if you're hoarding any really unnecessary items. I've never done this while actually living at home, so this one might actually be quite hard. You could, however, pack up some of your things for a while and see if you notice a difference after 30 days.

300. Rent your home with Airbnb

If I owned my own home, I'd definitely consider this, whether I was living there at the time or away on holiday. If you're unsure, you could try it out for 30 days and use the money to go on holiday.

301. Stop eating meals in front of the TV

When I read this one back it almost sounds preachy. There's nothing wrong with eating in front of the TV. But if you do it constantly, and you're barely tasting your food, then consider ditching TV eating for a month and see if you enjoy your food more.

302. Select new images for your home

I think the images you surround yourself with in your home are really important and work almost like subliminal messages. Take a look at what's around you and consider whether they're positive influences in your life. You could also use it as an opportunity to surround yourself with things you'd like to see more of in the future.

303. Collect interesting rocks for your garden or home

I like collecting interesting rocks when I'm on a beach, but I don't bother elsewhere. I'm sure pretty stones exist everywhere if you set your eyes to the task of finding them though. By the end of the month, you'll have a new rock collection to decorate around plant pots, your mantel piece, or big glass vases with candles.

304. Choose a different cupboard or drawer in your home to organise

Over time, I always end up with at least a few draws that just get filled with random junk. Depending on how messy you are, spend one month cleaning, tidying and making all cupboards and drawers in your house pristine.

305. Give away one thing a day that you don't need

If you're a bit of a hoarder, this one's for you or give away clothes you don't wear any more. Sell things you no longer need. Spreading this task out over a month or even longer, might make it easier to depart with your stuff.

306. Make natural products for your home

Make a list of the cleaning and beauty products you use the most such as shampoo, conditioner, surface cleaner etc, then research how to make natural alternatives. In the long run you could potentially save loads of money doing this and possibly help your skin if it often gets irritated by certain ingredients in cleaning and beauty products.

307. Feng Shui all rooms in your home
I read a bit about Feng Shui before I reorganised my bedroom and love how it looks and feels. You can go incredibly in depth into this subject, but the good news here is that you can alter a lot by rearranging a few things.

308. Keep your bed nicely made
My Grandma would often say, *"If you're bed is tidy, your room is tidy"*. Get into the habit of making your bed look good as soon as you wake up and it will be much more inviting when you go to bed at night.

309. Learn how to fix your car
Just a suggestion. If you use it daily, it might be useful to know how it works and what to do if it breaks down. At the very least, learn how to change a wheel. I have no firsthand experience here as I can't drive, but I have been in cars that have broken down and admired it when people were able to change wheels so efficiently.

310. Revamp your garden
Get weeding, decorate plant pots with stones, plant seeds, grow vegetables, make a mosaic pattern from colourful smashed tiles...there are loads of ways you can make your garden prettier without calling in a landscape gardener or buying exotic looking plants.

311. Make a small pond
With a bit of pond making research, some helpful volunteers, materials and digging, you could have a home for some new fish and frogs at the end of the month.

312. Make a wormery or insect hotel for your garden

If you've got kids, they might enjoy making this and it'll help to balance out your garden's ecosystem.

313. Make a home photo board

Cork, string, old fabric bed headboards — there are many ways you can make a photo board frame. You can then start to decorate with photos. I never really print photos out anymore, but I think houses always feels better with photos that make you feel good.

314. Make your bedroom a technology free zone

It depends how far you want to go with this one. You could take your TV out, or stop using your laptop on your bed. If you go to sleep next to your phone, you could move it away from your bed so it's not necessarily the first thing you look at when you wake up.

315. Create a space in your home for meditation and relaxation

A small room would be ideal, but a designated space would be just as good. You'll be more likely to keep up a regular meditation practice if you have somewhere relaxing to sit, that makes you feel good and is free from distractions.

316. Get a SAD lamp

I've heard good things about these lamps, but I've never used one myself. If you feel down in the cold winter months or you have Seasonal Affective Disorder[69], you could try using one of these for a month or borrowing one from a friend to see if it makes a difference.

317. Light candles

Light a candle a day to meditate on, focus on the things you're grateful for or set a daily intention whilst focusing on the fmale. Just remember not to forget about them.

318. Make art for your walls
There are loads of suggestions in the **recreation, art and creative chapter**, but don't think that because you can't draw or you think you're not good at art, you can't make beautiful things for your home yourself.

319. Fill your home with more plants
I once filled the office I was working in at the time with loads of plants and instantly felt better. If you don't have at least one plant in your house, I strongly advise you to get one, especially if you live in a polluted city. Some of the best plants for improving air quality include the bromeliad plant, dracaena and the spider plant[70].

320. Start a fire wood log collection
Since my parents moved to the countryside, one of my Dad's new hobbies has been to collect firewood. I don't have any first-hand experience with this one, but if you collect and chop it yourself, you'll be saving money and you'll probably enjoy your fires more.

321. Always recycle and compost food waste
Just in case you don't do it already, get yourself a recycling bin or start composting food waste rather than throwing it in with the rest of your rubbish.

322. Make a note of how much time you spend doing different everyday activities
Doing this for a whole month might test your patience, but you could see where and how you spend most of your time over the course of a week. Then spend the rest of your 30

day challenge reflecting on the information and seeing what (if any) changes you might make to create more balance in your life.

323. Mend old clothes
Sew up holes with thread, polish leather shoes to make them last longer, and sew new buttons onto worn jackets. I've often bought stuff from charity shops with missing buttons, and then transformed the item by just sewing some new buttons on.

324. Stop buying bottled water
Befriend the environment instead and get a reusable water bottle you can use again and again.

325. Organise everything you need the day before
Your mornings will feel so much better if you do this. Pack everything you need in your bag, make your lunch the day before, or even lay breakfast things out so they're ready for you in the morning. I've never managed to do this one, but it might help to make your mornings easier if you're very busy.

326. Collect interesting objects to grow plants in
Providing you do it right, you can get really creative with your plant pots. Grow plants in old shoes, bathtubs, or even instruments.

327. Keep a folder of food recipes
Make it your mission to find a new recipe a day, either from people you know, cutting recipes out of magazines or TV food programmes.

328. Make sure your house is tidy when you

return home

The last thing you want after a stressful day is to come home to a messy house with clutter everywhere. Give yourself a bit longer in the mornings to make sure breakfast things are always cleared away.

329. Hide all clutter

You don't have to go clinically minimalist but if you live in a pretty cluttered space, you could experiment first with a few rooms by storing excess things away in cupboards or pretty storage boxes. Do you really need everything on display?

Productivity at work 30 day challenges

330. Write out your three most important tasks for the day

I first tried this after during my Regus productivity challenge[71] and although I only did it for a week, it definitely helped to improve my productivity. Make this task one of the first things you do in the morning. It beats lengthy to do lists and from experience it works.

331. Check your emails only twice a day

I've had jobs in the past where I'd be really proud of myself for responding to emails straight away and I'd get really happy when people would reply back and say thank you for your quick response. In reality though, I was being completely unproductive and wasting time. If you're as bad as I was at responding straight away this one's for you. I first heard about this idea from the *Four Hour Work Week*[72], which I loved reading.

332. Go meeting free for a month

I've been in meetings before that have been solely about planning for the next meeting. I know this might be out of your control, but if you are someone who has the power to say "let's ditch meetings for a month" try it out. At the very least, see if you can cut the time you spend in meetings.

333. No work related conversations after work hours

I don't think there's anything wrong with talking about your work after work hours, but if you're complaining incessantly about your job at times when you could be relaxing or enjoying yourself with the people you're with, then maybe consider this one.

334. No office gossiping

I'm a big believer in this one. It creates such a toxic environment to work in, especially for new people who come in.

335. Tackle your most important tasks first

According to the book *The One Thing*[73], you're more likely to get important things done efficiently if you do them first. Certainly, don't complete important tasks when you're tired and drained of energy.

336. Come into work half an hour early

I used to work with a girl who did this. It was also one of my brother's suggestions. Their reasoning is that you get a head start on the day. I'm not saying I agree with it but if it resonates with you, maybe try it out for 30 days. Your boss might thank you for it.

337. Ditch working over-time

I like the Danish work philosophy of finishing on time every day. Overtime is something that is frowned upon there[74].

338. Quit complaining at work

I've had periods of complaining about jobs I've been in and it's never productive. You'll just end up disliking your work even more. Either find a solution and go with it or find a new job. When you carry on complaining, you end up draining everyone else's energy around you too.

339. Fill your office with more plants

In one of my old jobs, it took me about a month, to slowly fill our office with plants along the window sill. I have no idea what evidence there is for this one, but I honestly felt more productive with plants around me. Plus, it meant I was forced to take regular breaks, to water them all.

340. Practise meditating with your colleagues

I appreciate that everyone might not be up for this, but if you own a company, seriously consider getting someone to come in once a week to lead a meditation session tailored for your workplace. Once you all know what you're doing, it could become a regular way to start your day.

341. Limit social media use (unless it's your job)

I recently got into using Instagram, which started as a 'post a photo a day' 30 day challenge. However, the downside is that I started checking my phone way more than usual, which was completely unproductive and pointless. Perhaps, only use social media during working hours for a specific purpose and put a limit on the amount of times you look at your phone.

342. Try out the Pomodoro Technique by breaking your day into 25 min slots

When I was revising for exams, I used to find breaking my time into short slots helpful, but I don't have any experiencing of doing this in day-to-day life. If you have an issue with time management, give it a go and see if it works for you. This article, *The Pomodoro Technique: Is it right for you?*[75] Might be a good place to start.

343. Give up multitasking

It's a myth and it's not productive. If you really have to do multiple things, task switch instead. Never do two important things at once otherwise you'll end up doing those things badly and you'll make mistakes.

Career boosting and work 30 day challenges

344. Learn copywriting

Never think this is a skill only for advertisers and marketers. The world needs words and you probably use them more than you think. At the very least, being aware of fundamental copywriting techniques will help you write a CV and cover letter people will enjoy reading.

345. Offer your services on Freelance sites

There are loads of Freelance sites where you could offer your proofreading, editing, Photoshop, design...skills. *Guru, Freelancer* and *Upwork* might be good places to start.

346. Start teaching something you're good at

You might need to be qualified and accredited, but if you've got a lot of experience at something and you're passionate, people will definitely want to be taught by you. One of my good friends, used to teach people English over Skype.

347. Write a nonfiction or fiction ebook

I strongly recommend that you read Steve Scott's, *How to Write a nonfiction ebook in 21 days*[76]. It's helped me a lot with this one.

348. Get work experience

If you want to change careers, sample new ones by contacting places you like the sound of and going to work with them for either the whole 30 days, or pick out a selection of places to sample over the course of a month.

349. Talk to people who can help with your career

Phone, email or ask people in your existing circles for career advice, whether you're working for yourself or you're looking to change careers completely. Once you've gathered enough information, start implementing some of the ideas as a 30 day challenge.

350. Learn new skills on Lynda

In a way there's no excuse not to be able to do anything anymore. We can find pretty much anything out at the touch of a button. The same can be said for learning. Lynda is an online education company that offers free courses to help improve your tech, design, business skills and more.

351. What's the one thing you'd do every day for free? Write down steps and ideas for accomplishing it.

It might sound idealistic, but it's good advice. Why waste your life doing something you don't enjoy every day?

352. Start an Etsy or Not on the High Street shop

Definitely do this if you make things like art prints or jewellery. You can sell anything that's handmade by yourself. I felt inspired to start an Etsy shop with my Mum after doing a 30 day art challenge.

353. Buy a plant and hang nice quotes on it

You see stuff like this at specific events or open days, but it'd be nice just to have one in your office permanently.

354. Offer to do social media and digital marketing for companies

If you're looking for new freelancing ideas and you're good with social media, you could offer your services to small businesses who don't want to employ someone full time.

355. Grow fruit/veg in your office

I had a chilli plant in my office once. However, there's loads of fruit and veg you can grow indoors such as tomatoes, which also smell amazing as they're growing and taste good too if you don't put too much tomato feed on them.

356. Do lunchtime fitness sessions

It'd be great if all workplaces provided free fitness sessions to employees, especially if your job requires you to be sedentary. Working out for even just 10 minutes at lunch will give you energy, increase your productivity and hopefully stop you feeling drowsy in the afternoon.

Money and finance
30 day challenges

357. Recycle your stuff
Spend 30 days sorting through things in your life that you no longer need or use. Sell old clothes on eBay or receive money for recycling them. Sell old CDs, DVDs and other household items you no longer want or need.

358. Only buy things with cash
Give yourself a budget for the week, take out the cash, and then only use this money. It's really easy to overspend especially in supermarkets and shopping centres. I don't know if there's any proof in this, but It's helped me in the past, especially now it's so easy just to tap your card when you pay for things.

359. Ditch mainstream products
Go for the unbranded cereals, tins and shampoo. You can always go back after a month if the quality isn't as good. However, most of the time, the products are just as good, but half the price.

360. Find a good money management app
Record your daily, weekly or monthly spends, find out where you're overspending or create a plan to budget.

361. Double what you save each day
You could start with a really small amount such as one

pound or a penny and then the next day save two pounds, on the third day four, and so on. Then at the end of the month either save it or treat yourself.

362. Share with your neighbours
When I was younger, my parents used to share a lawn mower with the family next door. You could also share lifts if you work close together, especially if you consistently drive alone to work.

363. Put your pennies in a jar
You'll be more likely to find loose change if you do this. For example, I spotted two pound coins on the street this morning.

364. Can you turn £100 into £500 in a month or £500 into £5000?
I can't tell you what to do for this, but it could be an interesting challenge. What could you sell? What could you buy with £100 that would help you make £500? What would you do with the money at the end?

365. Stop wasting your food
According to *Love Food Hate Waste*[77], the average UK household wastes an average of £470 a year on food waste. Start looking at ways you could reduce your food waste now, and this could be a massive long term money saver for you.

366. Live on a strict budget for a month then splash out at the end
Cut down on meals out, walk or cycle to work, only buy things you need. If you never feel you have enough disposable income, you can treat yourself or someone you love at the end of the month with this one.

367. Start saving 10% of your income and love doing it

This one has helped me to save a lot more than I usually would since I started doing it, but I understand it's not for everyone. What I will say, is that no matter how much you're earning, it adds up and at the time, you really don't feel like you're missing out on the money.

368. Sell 30 things you don't need, use or wear anymore and see how much money you make at the end of the month

Most of us collect things we never use and allow them to gather dust. Spend a month clearing out all the things you never use that might be worth something.

369. Reflect on your attitude towards money

Sometimes it's our attitude that holds us back and money is no exception with this one. Do you believe money is a bad thing? Do you think you're worth more than you're currently earning? Do you think it's possible to make money doing what you love or would this make you feel guilty? Do we need money? Is it possible to live without it? Keep asking yourself questions like this and then adjust your attitude accordingly. Just make sure you're not short changing yourself because of an underlying negative attitude towards money.

370. Learn more about money through James Altucher

For those of you who don't know, he's an entrepreneur, investor and author of the book *Choose Yourself*[78] which I loved reading, to name just a few things. He's got lots of really good tips about money, work and being an entrepreneur through both his website and newsletter.

371. Be generous with your money

Being more generous with your money is supposed to get you into the mind-set that you have enough to give and as a result, you'll attract more money to you. It's up to you whether you believe in this one or not, but you could give it a go for a month and see. Use your judgement here. Maybe if you never give any of your money away and you have a lot of disposable income, experiment and see what it feels like to be more generous with it.

Intellectual and educational 30 day challenges

Art theory, languages and humanities
Science, technology and mathematics
Logic and memory
Misc education and learning

Art theory, languages and humanities 30 day challenges

372. Read a poem a day

Ask friends for their recommendations, search the web for poetry lists, or become familiar with the work of just one poet. You could form your reading list prior to your 30 day challenge so you know exactly what you're reading on each day, or you could keep it random and decide on a poem to suit your mood.

373. Read a book you wouldn't normally read

Read a novel from a genre you usually wouldn't read. Learn about something you know nothing about, or select a new book to read at random. There's a lot to be learnt from pushing yourself out of your comfort zone and reading something by someone with a completely different viewpoint to you.

374. Pick an art movement a day to inspire you

You don't have to be an art student for this one. Learning about different art movements can teach you so much about history, culture and society, as well as helping you to think more creatively — no matter what field you're in. There's a good book called *Isms: understanding art*[79], which takes you through some key art movements. Alternatively, write out your own list and research online.

375. Learn how to say common phrases in different languages

Select which languages you're going to use, then pick 30 common universal phrases such as hi, cheers and thank you. You'll be working your memory with this one, and you never know when it might help to break the ice with someone.

376. Read about a different period of history

If you're a British student who grew up in the 90s and didn't specialise in history, you'll probably know about the Celts, Romans, Victorians, Henry VIII, and WW2. But what about all the other important events in history throughout the world? You won't learn everything in a month, but you could swot up on 30 key periods of history in a month that weren't covered in your school's curriculum.

377. Become familiar with Edward de Bono's 6 thinking hats

Edward De Bono is the master of lateral thinking and developed something called the 'Six Thinking Hats', which is a genius way of making decisions effectively in group situations, or individually. Although there's lots of information freely available online, this book *Six Thinking Hats*[80] might be a good place to start. It was the first book I read by him.

378. Study a religious text in more detail or one you're not familiar with at all

Rediscover your own religion in a new way. Learn more about someone else's or understand why other people believe what they do.

379. Learn about different types of intelligence

When I studied applied philosophy and eastern psychology as part of my meditation teacher training, we talked quite extensively about this one. In the west, we tend to define intelligence as being intellectual or gifted academically. Or we like summing up what intelligence is in an IQ test or short statement, such as the ability to retain knowledge, being quick witted or being able to understand things quickly. What about other types of intelligence such as emotional, movement or spiritual? To start, you could read Howard Gardner's[81] work on different kinds of intelligence.

380. Learn how to use grammar correctly

I'm not a Grammar Nazi but I do like to see sentences being constructed correctly. It shouldn't take you that long to swot up on the basics. Choose one thing a day to focus on such as correct use of commas or semicolons and see how far you get in 30 days. Alternatively, find a Style Guide and spend a bit of time each day studying it.

381. Research prominent women throughout history

How many famous women poets, artists, scientists, political activists can you name? There are many out there, but many of us can name significantly more men than women.

382. Learn about a different historical person each day

Pick a subject or mix your niches, then select 30 people who interest you and spend a bit of time learning about what they did and why they're important historical figures.

383. Spend 30 minutes learning a new language

Unless you're highly skilled at languages, you probably won't learn a whole new language in a month, but you could certainly learn a lot. I've often found Michel Thomas language programs to be really good.

384. Learn a new alphabet

I'm not sure how long this one might take because I've never done it, but it's on here because quite a few people have suggested it to me. You could learn the Greek, Arabic or Hindi alphabets — to name just a few. Use it as a memory training exercise, or get creative with it and incorporate what you learn into artwork or calligraphy. My Dad, for example, spent 30 days learning the basics of the Greek alphabet so he could understand more Greek on holiday.

385. Study the language on TV news programmes

Pick a news programme or study a variety of different shows then listen carefully to the language being used and the stories that are reported. At the end of your 30 days see which words or phrases were being used the most, which stories were covered more than others and which ones weren't covered at all. See what you learned, at the end and if this changes your approach to the news.

386. Learn new things about your hometown

Once when I was away, someone asked me what the population of my hometown (Hull) was, and I didn't know for certain which was a bit embarrassing at the time. In case you're interested, it's 300,000. We can spend a lot of time exploring other cultures and visiting exotic lands, but what interesting or obvious things can you find out about your hometown in 30 days?

387. Study different newspapers to find out which subjects are covered most

Similar to studying different news programmes, select a few different newspapers and look at the types of stories covered. How do the stories differ from newspaper to newspaper? How varied is the language? Are certain words used more than others?

388. Learn a quote a day
Select 30 quotes that mean something to you, put them into a hat and pick a quote out a day to learn. Choose a specific theme such as 'feel good' or thought provoking', or be completely random for a surprise. You could also ask other people for their quote suggestions.

389. Travel locally and see what you learn
Buy your local guide book, and seek out places of interest that you haven't been to before in your hometown or local area. If you complain a lot about where you live, this one's for you. There have to be some perks. The *Lonely Planet* might be good for this as they often include hidden little places you might not even know exist.

390. Learn a new word a day
How extensive is your vocabulary? Pick words at random from a dictionary or read the book *500 words you should know*[82] by Caroline Taggart. It won't take up much of your time to learn one new word a day.

391. Place post it notes with new words from a different language all over your house
We have post it notes on our fridge in Spanish. Providing the people you're living with don't mind, if you're learning a new language, you could place post it notes all over — next to everyday objects such as the light switches, doors, cups, kettle, etc.

392. Visit a church, temple or other religious building

Whether you're religious or not, most churches and temples allow people from all walks of life to enter. Everyone will have their own reasons for this one. Maybe you're a Christian but you haven't found a church to go to regularly. Maybe you're confused by religion and want to gain a deeper understanding. Maybe you're just looking for a place to meditate or connect with God.

393. Research ancient laws in your country that still exist

In the UK, for example, it's illegal to put washing lines up across a street and to place a postage stamp bearing the Queen's head, upside down.

394. Research a different Hindu God each day

Each God represents something different and has a story to tell. For example, Ganesha — the elephant God represents overcoming obstacles, Shiva is known as the destroyer and Brahma is known as the creator. I'm oversimplifying, but you get the idea.

395. Learn about politics

Each day, give yourself something new to learn, either studying the history of politics in your country over the last 40-50 years, learning about the different political parties whilst also questioning your own beliefs and values, or find someone who's pretty clued up already and get them to create a rough outline of what to study.

396. Study different philosophers

Expand on your existing knowledge, study one philosopher for 30 days, or choose 30 philosophers and learn about each one briefly. You could then go into more depth with the philosophers that interest you.

397. Learn about psychology studies

Choose 30 psychology studies from the last 100 years and spend a month reading briefly about each one. You could pick a theme or research the most famous experiments.

398. Learn about a new country a day

Discover who the leader of the country is, what the cost of living is, or what people from that country enjoy eating. Either look up different facts for each country or select a theme such as fashion, art or celebrating the New Year.

399. Put a pin on a world map and learn about that place

If you were learning about different countries, you could choose them with pins. With this one, you're being more specific, researching into a specific town city or ocean — wherever the pin lands.

400. Research a different culture's attitude towards marriage

I haven't done this one, but I think it'd be fascinating. Find out where marriages are the strongest, how weddings are traditionally celebrated, and where the tradition originated and why according to the culture.

401. Find out how different cultures express themselves through art

Pick a culture or subculture and look at how they express themselves currently through art. Either look at the history or present day art of that culture. If you're an artist, it might really help to inspire your own work.

402. Listen to music from a different

country each day
Pick 30 countries and spend a month listening to new bands and artists from around the world.

403. Learn about a new religion
Learn about the major religions that exist today over the course of a month, or pick one religion to learn about in more depth.

404. Research love
I know this sounds strange, but I think it'd be a really lovely 30 day project. Discover art that centres around love, read love poems, find out what love means to different people, look at different quotes on love...Keep the theme open, or get really specific — the choice is yours.

405. Reflect on what God means to you
Regardless of who you are — whether you're religious, atheist, agnostic or unsure, spend a month to reflect on what God means to you, if there is a God at all, or why people might believe or not believe in a God. This could help to make your own views clearer or make you more understanding of what other people believe.

406. Learn about Ayurveda
Ayurveda is a natural medical system that comes from India and is still used today. While you certainly won't learn everything in a month, you can definitely learn the basics and learn more about your dosha type. Are you more vata, pitta or kapha?

Science, technology and mathematics 30 day challenges

407. Learn anatomy through drawing the body

If you have to learn anatomy for a particular course you're doing, visually learning through drawing, might really help. Find a local anatomy drawing class, seek out online tutorials or copy pictures from your existing anatomy book. Focus on drawing a different section of the body a day.

408. Use the Khan Academy

You can learn maths, science, economics, computer programming and much more online, for free. It's probably one of the best online learning systems I've come across.

409. Read about multiverse theories

Write down a few of the theories, then spend 30 days finding out as much as you can about the multiverse.

410. Teach yourself economics

Economics is one of those subjects so many of us know little about. It's not compulsory to learn it at school in the UK at all, yet it's such an important subject and affects all of our lives. Spending a month learning some of the basics could be really fascinating. Just make sure you study this in a balanced way, so your judgments aren't skewed by one economist's point of view.

411. Teach yourself basic Maths

Maths was never my strong point at school. Skip this if you're already a maths genius, but if you're not spend a month teaching yourself some basic maths skills. Using the Khan Academy might be a good place to start, and the learning will be fun.

412. Use the Brain and/or Anatomy Colouring Book[83]

During my meditation teacher training, I had to study the basics of the brain and found this book incredibly useful. You colour in different sections of the brain as you learn and it's suitable for all levels and abilities.

413. Learn about prominent scientists throughout history

Most of us probably know a bit about Einstein, Newton and Darwin, but can you talk a bit about 30 different scientists? Pick a theme within science, or select people at random. Alternatively, go into more depth and just choose one scientist that interests you.

414. Take things apart and put them back together

My brother used to do this one a lot whilst growing up. If you're into electronics, you're probably doing this already, but if you're not, it might help you figure out how to fix things when they break.

415. Build yourself a computer

You could save yourself a lot of money if you do this one. Just find out which parts you need, order them online, then seek out a reputable guide if you're unsure how to go about doing this. I've been told it's easy, but have never tried this one.

416. Learn the periodic table
Find fun ways to memorise the periodic table such as through Tom Lehrer's *Elements* song[84], then learn about the properties of each element in more depth. See how far you get in 30 days.

417. Solve a maths problem
Ask someone you know who's quite savvy with maths to create a problem for you to solve in a month. Alternatively, seek out 30 appropriate maths challenges to do over a month.

418. Teach yourself basic computer programming
It's unlikely you'll be an expert in a month, but you will certainly learn a lot from an online course

419. Keep a notebook of invention ideas
Write down all your ideas for a month, even if they sound mad. One day you might reread your list, if not during your 30 day challenge, and stumble across something that might actually be useful. Alternatively, consistently ask yourself 'what does the world need?' then write out your daily suggestions.

420. Reflect on consciousness
Some questions to reflect on over a month could be, what does consciousness mean to you? Is consciousness something unique to humans? How did consciousness evolve? Jot your thoughts down in a notebook, find theoretical books to read, or meditate on different possibilities.

421. Learn about different kinds of renewable energy

Find out which countries use the most renewable energy. How many types of renewable energy systems are there and which ones are the most useful? Is it possible to be entirely renewable with our energy one day? Ask yourself specific questions each day, make a list of different renewable energy systems to find out about, or discover all you can about one type of energy system such as offshore wind farms or solar power.

422. Research the placebo effect

Find out about existing placebo effect experiments, research the power of belief and how that relates to the placebo effect, or find a good book on the subject. If the placebo effect works, shouldn't we all be learning how to harness the power of our minds to self-heal?

423. Design a simple app

Come up with some basic ideas and start building. Treat this more as a problem-solving project rather than trying to create the next big app out there.

Logic and memory
30 day challenges

424. Do Sudoku or crosswords

Get yourself a cheap Sudoku book and aim to do one a day to improve your concentration, enhance memory and possibly lower your chances of getting certain degenerative diseases in old age.

425. Play brain games

There are a lot of free games on Lumosity that help to improve your cognitive skills. I got into playing *Word Bubbles* and *Tetris* for a while. In terms of research, senior researcher, Jane McGonigal discovered that playing Tetris can help to prevent PTSD[85].

426. Improve your memory with chunking

The average person is able to hold between five to nine pieces of information in their short-term memory[86]. See if you can learn how to hold more information in yours using chunking. In a nutshell, chunking allows you to remember a lot more by allowing you to chunk groups of information together. For example, people who remember huge food orders in restaurants are probably using chunking.

427. Play chess

It's creative, it improves your memory and helps you to think strategically. You could play this on your phone on the way to work if you use public transport and you've got a lengthy commute.

428. Put a jigsaw together

As well as being incredibly therapeutic to do in times of stress, putting together a jigsaw will give your problem-solving skills a boost as well as keeping your mind active and alert. Plus, if you choose a picture you like, you can always get your jigsaw framed for your home. Or you could take on a 3D jigsaw.

429. Answer general knowledge questions

You could put loads of general knowledge questions in a hat and then pick a few out each day. Or, spend five to ten minutes a day learning random facts and get really good at pub quizzes.

430. Solve IQ questions

Select a few IQ questions every day to solve. Find a balance between general mental ability questions and abstract reasoning ones. You could complete an IQ test prior to and after your 30 day challenge to see how you've progressed if this is possible. Or just complete the questions for the fun of it.

431. Get better at object perception by throwing stuff

This was one of my Uncle Doug's suggestions. Just make sure you've got enough space to do this. You don't want to start smashing your crockery collection. All you have to do for this one is throw stuff then guess how far you've thrown it. You can then see how good your object perception is after each guess.

432. Memorise countries and/ or capital cities

There are 196 countries in the world. All you need to do is memorise six to seven a day and you'll have them all in a month. Use the *Sporcle, Countries of the World Game* to test your knowledge. You can then move onto capital cities. The site *Memorize* will help to get you started.

433. Memorise past presidents/ prime ministers from your country

How many famous presidents or prime ministers from your country can you name? Make it your mission to learn a president a day along with the political party they belonged to plus a few small facts about them.

434. Memorise Greek gods and goddesses

The artwork is stunning and you might find the stories beautiful to learn about as well as improving your memory.

Misc education and learning 30 day challenges

435. Read an article on a different subject

Ditch your main source of news for a month and seek out good quality pieces of journalism on different subjects. You could cover 30 subjects in 30 days or you could focus on the same subject every day and read articles with different points of view. This is a good one if you consistently read articles on only one subject area or viewpoint.

436. Play devil's advocate with yourself

Write out your opinions on a wide variety of issues ranging from politics to art — and then spend 30 days playing devil's advocate with yourself. Where did your original opinion come from in the first place? Record your answers in a journal. Alternatively, if you're quite opinionated as a person, over the course of a month, keep a record each day of when you expressed a strong opinion about something. It could be commenting on a news article or responding to something someone has said. You can then question your beliefs as and when. This is more an exercise in helping you to form opinions that have substance.

437. Take note of everyday life lessons

If you're open to it, see if you can learn a new lesson every day. Rather than actively going out searching for knowledge, see what naturally comes your way. Learn from books or articles that come into your path, observing others, failures and your own reaction to things.

438. Become interested in something you've never shown an interest in

It could be rugby, botany, horoscopes, 20th century literature or car mechanics. Pick a new subject each day or swot up on one thing for a month. Don't pick a subject you'll hate learning about just for the sake of it. The idea is to discover something you never knew you liked.

439. Learn something new from everyone you meet

I'm a big believer in this one. Aim to really listen, engage and connect with everyone you come across — even if the meeting is brief. It might be easier if you write your thoughts down in a journal. It could be knowledge, someone's attitude to life, how someone makes you feel. Pay attention and you will be given gems of knowledge and wisdom everywhere you go

440. Pick a subject you're interested in and develop really niche knowledge within that subject

For example, if you're into gardening, could you develop really niche knowledge for a particular type of plant or if you're into art, find out as much as you can about one painting.

Social, relationship and kindness
30 day challenges

Social and relationships
Everyday kindness to yourself, others and the planet

Social and relationship 30 day challenges

441. Speak to someone new
It could be someone you've never spoken to at work, someone serving you at the bar or the person you're sitting next to on the bus.

442. Eat with people you care about
Can you sit down with people you love and eat one meal every day together for 30 days?

443. Be more assertive
This is something I've often struggled with and admire anyone who can get the balance right without sounding rude. For this one, think about people you know who do assertiveness really well and ask them for tips, or think about what it is that makes them assertive. You don't need to go out of your way looking for ways to assert yourself for this challenge — just set the intention to be more assertive and see where it takes you.

444. Strike up a conversation with a stranger while you're waiting for something
If you find yourself in queues quite a lot or you spend time waiting for something every day, seek out one person to talk with.

445. Hold eye contact with a stranger for longer than five seconds
This was one of my brother's suggestions. It might feel weird at first, but it's led to him meeting loads of interesting

people. If you do this one, make sure you don't accidentally scare anyone!

446. Befriend someone on the bus or train

My Grandma always chats to people when she's on the bus. I don't see why we all shouldn't try this — even if it's just for a month. You never know who you might end up talking to.

447. Remember the names of new people

I've often been rubbish at remembering people's names but I'm getting better. Mentally repeating the person's name after you've been introduced helps, and so does associating that person with something. For example, on my yoga teacher training, my teacher Mimi managed to recall all 20 of our names instantly after asking us what our names were and our favourite food.

448. Improve your conversational skills

Sometimes I feel I'm better at expressing myself through writing, but give me the right conversation with the right people and I'm happy. This one isn't about reading some tried and tested formula — it's more about observing yourself when you're having conversations and improving in areas that make you feel uncomfortable. What do you mainly talk about with people? Are you mostly serious? When was the last time you made someone laugh? What can you do to improve your small talk or completely avoid it? Which conversations make you want to run away and why?

449. Take it in turns to cook

Start a cooking rota as a family, partner, with your housemates or even as a community. If you swap meals with other households locally, you'll get to try new kinds of food.

450. Eat together at the dinner table

I don't believe in any right or wrong way to eat, but if you never do this — give it a go for a month, even if it's just a few times a week. When you're in a family and you all have different interests, dinner time is often the place you can all sit and be together.

451. Treat everyone you meet as a potential new friend

People do this when they're travelling alone, and you can meet some of the best people with this mind-set. I don't see why this one can't be done wherever you are though.

452. Talk less. Listen more

Observe yourself when you talk with people. How often do you interrupt? Are you really listening or waiting for your moment to speak? What happens when you start talking less and listening more?

453. Talk more

Observe yourself when you're with others. How often do you stay quiet when you feel you have something valuable to add to a conversation? Are you quiet because you're afraid to speak or because you're more interested in listening? Don't stop listening, but just observe and see what happens when you start talking more if it's something you want to do.

454. Teach yourself to get good at public speaking

This would have to be one of my biggest fears and I know I'm not alone. I don't have any practical advice, but I've heard good things about *Toastmasters*, which is a global organisation that helps people to be better communicators, leaders and public speakers.

455. Spend time with people you like

This one might seem strange because why would you spend

time with people you don't like, but I guess we do this one all the time. We stay in touch with people who put us down, we eat lunch with colleagues that irritate us, or we become a sounding board for people to offload. It might seem harmless, but people like this are energy drainers. Observe how many people are like this in your life and then re-evaluate who you spend the majority of your time with.

456. Seek to understand others' motives

People might make passive aggressive comments when they're secretly feeling insecure, or react explosively when they need help. Rather than fighting fire with fire, seek to understand someone's behaviour or motive for behaving in a certain way rather than lashing out.

457. Be completely selfless in your relationship

This one is from my friend Lily. If you always have your own way and have started to take your partner for granted, treat him or her to this. The only rule is that you can't tell your partner what you're doing. So, for 30 days, be more selfless — make them tea, be grateful for little things they do, give more, listen more, be the one to stop arguments if it gets to that or do small gestures to make their life easier. Just make sure you don't end up going to the other extreme and become a pushover.

458. Give your partner space

I was given this advice by someone I did meditation with. He said this helped his marriage a lot. When you give someone space, you allow them to be who they are. Whereas if you're too wrapped up in one another, there's a danger of losing part of your identity — especially if you stop doing the things you used to enjoy.

459. Write out 30 questions each with your

partner

Write out a list of 30 questions each that you want to know about each other and spend a month getting to know one another on a whole new level. This is a bit like *Truth or Dare* without the dare, unless you want to add it in too.

460. Switch roles in your relationship

If one of you always cooks for the other more or takes on the role of organiser, try switching for a month and see how it affects your relationship. It might be frustrating, but it might also help you to appreciate each other more.

461. Swap hobbies with someone

Spend time doing the stuff you each love for a month. I've never actually done this even though I've thought it'd be interesting.

462. Write your own personal relationship 30 day challenge

Each day, try something new with your partner — Write out 30 ideas that you'll both love and spend a month putting them into play. Examples could be going on a spontaneous weekly date, cooking together or something as simple as being there for them.

Everyday kindness to yourself, others and the planet 30 day challenges

463. Give back to the planet

Write out 30 things you can do each day to be kinder to the planet such as picking up litter, not drinking from takeaway coffee cups, planting trees and flowers or volunteering for an environmental charity. You can then spend 30 days implementing them.

464. Show others your true self

You don't need to go blurting out all your secrets, but there's a lot to be said for feeling at ease around people without worrying what they think of you. I know this is a lot harder in practise, but try giving more of yourself, especially around people you're usually closed off to. You might be surprised.

465. Give up your seat if you commute by train

In London, people can be really pushy to get on trains when it comes to rush hour. It's always really heartening when someone offers someone their seat when the train is packed full of people.

466. Buy homeless people hot drinks

Buy 30 hot drinks in 30 days or volunteer for a homeless charity.

467. Send a postcard to an old friend

Who doesn't like receiving postcards and handwritten

letters? Keep some stamps and spare postcards in your bag and write a letter a day to someone new. If you think this is time consuming, reflect on how much time you spend browsing on social media sites.

468. Give a compliment a day
You could really help to make someone's day. Just make sure you're genuine. People can tell when it's fake.

469. Give useful ideas to people
This was one of my brother's suggestions. If you've got skills or knowledge to impart, give people you know ideas or help — that's if they want it of course.

470. Volunteer for a cause you believe in
Work at a hospice, volunteer at a farm or work with the elderly or homeless. You don't even need to volunteer for a charity — how about helping out one of your neighbours?

471. Give people good hugs
You don't have to stand out in the street wearing a sign that says free hugs, but you could become more aware of how you hug people you're close to. We can all tell the difference between a heartfelt hug and one that's just for show or good manners. Make it your mission for a month to always hug people like you mean it.

472. Write nice/ funny made up horoscopes for people
If someone you know needs cheering up, it might be a nice thing to do for them. I don't have any experience of this, but it'd make me smile.

473. Give away books you no longer need
Write nice messages in the front of the books and give them

away to friends or leave them in public places for strangers to pick up.

474. Write out and do 30 different random acts of kindness

These could be simple things like helping someone with their shopping, thanking someone who wouldn't normally be thanked for the work they do or buying someone who needs it a hot drink.

475. Get involved with or start a local activist group

If your activism ends at posting something up on social media, find others who share your cause and find alternative ways to make a difference in addition to sharing things online.

476. Do karma yoga (selfless service) for at least 15 mins a day

Karma yoga is basically doing one good deed a day or selfless action. This could be anything from cleaning floors to serving food or just making people you care about cups of tea.

477. Spend 30 days fundraising for a charity or cause of your choice

Join an existing event or make your own up for a charity that's dear to your heart.

478. Write down something you love about your partner every day and give them the list after your month is up

Even if it sounds cheesy, doesn't everyone like hearing lovely things about themselves? You never know, it might end up being a really good 30 line love poem, even if you just end up being sarcastic with it and making them laugh.

479. Make someone a 30 song playlist
Even if you're bad at the art of playlist creating, you've got plenty of time to carefully plan each song.

480. Don't check your phone when you're with people
You might not even realise how much you do this one until you make an effort to stop. The people around you, even if they're not close friends or family, will really appreciate it. In a time when we're all glued to our phones, we need human connection more than ever.

481. Look after other people's pets while they're away
If you're an animal lover and you've got the space and time, definitely do this. I'm sure most pet owners would prefer to take their dog or cat to a warm, friendly home than a kennel or cattery. Even if you charged a bit of money, it'd still be a nice thing to do. My parents used to look after other people's dogs through the Yorkshire company *Holidays4Dogs*.

482. Send appreciation notes and tweets
Find one thing a day to appreciate and write or send a tweet that shows your gratitude. It could be to a person who has done something nice, a note to someone you love but have taken for granted recently, or it could be completely random like a note left on a window saying 'I appreciate this beautiful view'.

483. Speak kindly about people
I love hearing people saying genuinely kind things about others. Next time you feel like you might start to gossip or

bad mouth someone, see if you can turn it around and say something constructive instead.

484. Give people your full attention

How many of us really do this? Obviously, don't let people drain your energy, but try making eye contact more, being fully present when people talk to you, and making people feel valued. Every now and again I'll meet someone who's an incredible listener and it'll make me think about how well I listen and how often we get distracted as humans when we're interacting with others. People can sense it when you're really tuned into them — it's a really wonderful gift to give to someone.

485. Thank, tip or give small presents to people who aren't expecting it

We may be accustomed to tip at restaurants, but who else are you grateful for that you wouldn't normally thank? Try to find one person a day and show them that you appreciate the work they're doing.

486. Treat everyone with the same respect

Do you secretly look down on people you think aren't as good as you or suck up to those in a higher position? Even if you think you don't do this, observe your behaviour around everyone and make your own mind up.

487. Be the one to end gossipy conversations

It starts with one person gossiping about someone, and then someone else in that group agrees or adds their bit, or worse influences everyone else to think the same and then people bond over mutual gossiping, which to me is really wrong. I always respect people, who end bitchy cycles like this.

488. Leave food in your garden for birds

Rather than throwing away food scraps, you could give it to the birds — just make sure it's suitable for them to eat. Who doesn't enjoy seeing birds through the kitchen window?

489. Get to know your neighbours

Give yourself a month to get to know more of your neighbours. In big cities like London, people can live for years in a place without knowing their next-door neighbours' names.

490. Introduce your friends/acquaintances/contacts to one another

In your circle of friends, acquaintances and contacts, who could you introduce? Do you know someone who is an expert in their field and someone else who is trying to break into that field? Introduce them. Or just two people you feel would really benefit from knowing one another.

491. See the good in people

This doesn't mean ignoring the undesirable things in others, it just means giving people more of a chance, so you can see more of the good in them.

492. Give away some of your things for free

If you've just cleared out your wardrobe, give away items to friends who you think that piece of clothing would suit. If you're clearing out food cupboards, donate items to a food bank. Could you give away old furniture to a family who might really benefit from it?

493. Try WWOOFING

WWOOF stands for Worldwide Opportunities on Organic Farms. This might not be practical for everyone, but there might be opportunities near to where you live if you have some time to give.

494. Switch cynicism for skepticism

I often feel people lump cynicism and skepticism in the same category but they're two very different things. I'm a massive advocate for being skeptical but hate cynicism. I feel that cynicism leads to lost opportunities whereas scepticism allows you to carefully examine what's in front of you so you can make the best possible decisions.

495. Try tithing

This is an ancient Christian idea which one of my friends has started doing and involves giving away 10% of your income to something you believe in. As a result, you're also supposed to benefit a lot from doing it.

496. Make decisions from your inner self not ego

There's a big difference here. Ego based decisions will never make you happy in the long run. I believe if more people made inner self based decisions, the world would be a more thoughtful, compassionate place. If you're unsure, which decisions are ego based and which ones come from your inner self, question your motives and really make an effort to tune into how you feel when you make decisions. What is your heart trying to say?

497. Be a person of action *and* words

We all want to hear lovely things and be told how wonderful we are. But these words are empty if there are no actions to back them up. Watch your behaviour in your relationships with people and observe your action/word balance.

498. Remember little things people say

I'm always touched when I meet a friend of a friend, and I

see them after a half a year or longer and they've remembered certain details from the last conversation we had. It might seem small, but this one will really mean a lot to people.

499. Be a humble person

If you're obsessed with status and fancy job titles and your ego has become a bit inflated, reflect on being humble for a month. This isn't the same as having low self-esteem.

500. Leave a note for a stranger to discover

I once discovered a note taped to a bus stop in Surbiton, telling me to seize the day and make it amazing, followed by #footprintsofkindness. You could do something similar — write out 30 thoughtful notes and leave them in public places to make people smile, laugh or think.

Bonus material

30 thought provoking questions for 30 days

1. Who are you?

2. Which fictional character would you be and why?

3. Do you believe in a God or a higher power? If so, why or why not?

4. What would you do without fear?

5. If you could be an animal for a day, what would you choose and why?

6. What and who inspires you?

7. If you could spread one message or good idea, what would it be?

8. What do you spend most of your time thinking about?

9. What have been your happiest moments in life?

10. Is it possible to get rid of the ego?

11. What is the universe?

12. Is reincarnation possible?

13. How might you make the world a more peaceful place?

14. What lies behind the mind?

15. What's the one thing you've been putting off? Do it today.

16. If you're not your thoughts, things, interests, opinions, what are you?

17. If you had to change one thing about yourself (if anything) today, what might it be?

18. What is love?

19. What excites you?

20. What can you do today to help others more?

21. Will science eventually explain everything?

22. What happens when a person dies?

23. When and why did religion begin?

24. Where would you like to be in five years' time

25. Imagine being at your own funeral. What might people say about you?

26. What is the secret to a lasting relationship?

27. What is past present and future?

28. Is it possible for love to last forever?

29. How would you live your life or what would you do differently if no one was judging you?

30. What are you going to do today to be kind to yourself?

Original 30 day challenge list of 100 ideas from my blog

100 30 day challenge ideas to turn your life around

This was the blog post I wrote in 2014 on my website Thought Brick, which is the most read article on my site and as a result, inspired me to create this book of 500 30 day challenges. All the ideas here have been featured in the book, but here's the original list of 100 30 day challenge ideas listed randomly.

1. Take a photo a day on your way to work

2. Give a compliment a day

3. Speak to someone new every day

4. Keep a thought journal

5. Write your dreams down every morning for 30 days

6. Give up alcohol for a month

7. Give up TV for a month

8. Listen to a new song every day

9. Spend five minutes focusing on your breath every day

10. Take time out each day to watch your thoughts play out like a film — observing without judgement

11. Be totally honest — so no lying for 30 days

12. Draw or paint a picture a day

13. Learn something new every day

14. Teach others something new every day

15. Think of your worst habit, you've been meaning to ditch and give it up for 30 days

16. Drink eight glasses of water a day

17. Try hot yoga every day — many studios offer an intro discount!

18. Ditch the news for a month and instead seek out an interesting article to read every day

19. Cook or bake something new each day

20. Spend five minutes a day repeating a positive affirmation you've set yourself

21. Keep a laughter journal. Write down one thing a day that made you really laugh hard

22. Go for a 15 minute run every day

23. Do 50 sit-ups a day

24. Write a handwritten letter or send a postcard a day to old friends

25. Learn a dance routine as part of a group

26. Cycle to work

27. Write down a positive thought a day

28. Keep a gratitude list for 30 days

29. Before you go to sleep, think about the best thing that happened to you that day for five minutes

30. What have you always wanted to do but never have? Spend 30 days writing down ideas for accomplishing your goal

31. Spend at least five minutes doing laughter yoga every day

32. Knit a scarf in a month doing a few lines a day

33. Drink green tea (high in antioxidants) every morning

34. Give up bitching for a month or saying anything negative about people

35. Write a book in a month with help from National Novel Writing Month

36. Go money free or live on a strict budget for a month then splash out at the end

37. Wake up at 6am to meditate every morning

38. Play devil's advocate with yourself each day and really examine your own beliefs.

39. Face a new fear a day — talk to a stranger, pick up a

spider... push yourself out of your comfort zone

40. Learn to love yourself just a little bit more each day. You deserve it

41. Become a master of magic and learn a trick a day — just watch some YouTube videos.

42. Watch a film a day

43. Take a photograph of your food every day — it might force you to prepare nicer looking meals

44. Experiment wearing a new outfit every day

45. Plant a flower a day — in your garden or just in random places

46. Do karma yoga (selfless service) for at least 15 mins a day

47. Take up a new interesting hobby — tai chi, free running, pottery...

48. Write loads of cool ideas for things to do in a hat and pull out a different thing each day

49. Tell someone you love them each day

50. Text, write, message...people you care about and tell them why they're important to you

51. Learn to draw the human face — record your progress in a sketchbook and be amazed at the results

52. Take up life drawing

53. Learn a new instrument in a month — the ukulele, cello, flute — whatever takes your fancy

54. Bring your own lunch to work.

55. Be the 'Yes' man for a month and start saying yes to stuff

56. Stop smoking for 30 days.

57. Create a postcard sized piece of art each day and have a work of art to display at the end of the month.

58. Make a patchwork quilt in a month with 30 squares

59. Research a different religion or philosophy every day for a month

60. Read about a different period of history every day

61. Get knowledgeable about art and pick an art movement a day to inspire you

62. Do one thing each day that makes you feel inspired

63. Live in an ashram for a month or visit a temple every day

64. Revamp your house in a month and learn one upcycling trick a day

65. Learn a new word every day

66. Spend 30-60 mins practising a new language

67. If you live in a city, try to spend some time each day in nature whether it's your garden, a park or the countryside

68. Do an hour of exercise a day

69. Go on a date with yourself or partner doing something new each day

70. Make an item of jewellery a day

71. Cut out the caffeine for a month

72. Learn to lucid dream in 30 days

73. Ditch social media sites for 30 days, or limit yourself to a few minutes a day

74. Spend 30 days being a vegetarian or vegan

75. Eat something you've never tried before every day

76. Do an act of kindness a day

77. Go without talking for a month or visit a silent retreat

78. Visit a new website a day

79. Go internet free for a month

80. Donate a bit of money to charity every day

81. Read a chapter of a book a day

82. Spend a month reading the Bible

83. Research a different Hindu God each day

84. Make a 30 page hand drawn comic book in a month

85. Ditch your car for a month

86. Be positive for 30 days — even when things go wrong, look only for the positives

87. Try out napping in the afternoon or changing your regular sleeping patterns

88. Spend 30 days fundraising for a charity or cause of your choice

89. Go on a 30 day bike ride and see how far you get

90. Spend 30 days eating (healthy) raw food meals

91. Do a brain training puzzle a day like Sudoku, crosswords or anything Lumosity.

92. Feel beautiful in your own skin every day

93. Create a bucket list of 30 items in 30 days

94. Write down something you love about your partner every day and give them the list after your month is up

95. Read a poem a day

96. Write a poem a day

97. Dance every day — whether you're good at it or not

98. Don't buy anything new for a month

99. Sell 30 things you don't need, use or wear anymore and see how much money you make at the end of the month

100. Spend each day being as 'present' as possible and making the most of simple acts and routine tasks. Life will feel brighter and you will hopefully feel more fulfilled It's not often what we've got or where we are, but our attitude to what life throws our way.

A-Z of all 30 day challenges by category

Art theory, languages, and humanities (p102)

Read a poem a day
Read a book you wouldn't normally read
Pick an art movement a day to inspire you
Learn how to say common phrases in different languages
Read about a different period of history
Become familiar with Edward De Bono's 6 thinking hats
Study a religious text in more detail or one you're not familiar with at all
Learn about different types of intelligence
Learn how to use grammar correctly
Research prominent women throughout history
Learn about a different historical person each day
Spend 30 minutes learning a new language
Learn a new alphabet
Study the language on TV news programs
Learn new things about your hometown
Study different newspapers to find out which subjects are covered most
Learn a quote a day
Travel locally and see what you learn
Learn a new word a day
Place post it notes with new words from a different language all over your house
Visit a church, temple or other religious building
Research ancient laws in your country that still exist
Research a different Hindu God each day
Learn about politics
Study different philosophers
Learn about psychology studies

Learn about a new country a day
Put a pin on a world map and learn about that place
Research a different culture's attitude towards marriage
Find out how different cultures express themselves through art
Listen to music from a different country each day
Learn about a new religion
Research love
Reflect on what God means to you
Learn about Ayurveda

Beauty, pampering and body image (p23)

Work on creating a positive self image
Ditch gossip magazines
Steam your face
Have cold showers
Use coconut oil
Ditch some of your beauty products
Spend up to five minutes looking into your own eyes in the mirror
Don't look in the mirror
Use luxurious ethical products that make you feel good
Go make-up free
Try out different make-up techniques
Stop sleeping with your make-up on
Massage your feet for two minutes every night before bed
Gently massage under your eyes
Try wearing natural deodorant
Learn to love yourself just a little bit more each day
Reorganise your wardrobe and wear a new outfit
Floss
Hold yourself well
Try Ayurveda oil pulling
Stop spending so much time on your appearance
Wear clothes with nice fabric
Stop shaving/ waxing your body hair

Make a homemade skin exfoliator
Develop your inner confidence
Live according to your Ayurvedic dosha type
Connect your skin with the earth

Creative (drawing, painting and sculpture) (p58)

Draw a postcard sized picture every day
Learn to draw faces
Learn to draw in sight-size
Draw with your eyes closed
Draw with your opposite hand
Learn to sculpt with clay
Draw something upside down
Draw on scrap bits of paper
Make rubbings of interesting surfaces and textures
Make a sculpture from random objects
Learn how to draw sacred geometry
Learn to carve things from wood
Draw using a Spirograph
Creature a miniature 'junk art' sculpture
Try free drawing
Make a 30 page hand drawn comic book
Doodle
Create a painting in a month
Paint a canvas in one colour
Paint a mural
Make land art
Try action painting
Collect paint sample strips and make art with them
Spend 20 minutes working on a piece of mandala artwork
Spend 15 minutes colouring every day
Make dictionary art
Design tattoos

Drink and food (p18)

Drink a pint of hot water with lemon and ginger first thing in the morning

Eat at least five pieces of fruit and veg every day

Drink green tea (high in antioxidants) every morning

Present your food nicely

Make spontaneous meals with limited ingredients

Try out a new diet

Don't drink caffeine after midday

Cook a meal you've never made before

Swap unhealthy snacks for healthy ones

Be aware of what you're really eating

Try eating at different times

Try out being a vegetarian or vegan

No eating out for 30 days

Grow your own Scoby and make your own kombucha

Make and eat your own fresh bread

Train yourself to like foods you don't usually have a taste for

Invent a new food or drink recipe

Cook with turmeric

Eat garlic and ginger

Cook lunches for the week ahead on Sunday

Eat colourful meals

Slow down your eating

Think good thoughts when you eat

Education and learning misc (p116)

Read an article on a different subject

Play devil's advocate with yourself

Take note of everyday life lessons

Become interested in something you've never shown an interest in

Learn something new from everyone you meet

Pick a subject you're interested in and develop really niche knowledge within that subject

Exercise and fitness (p16)

Train for a triathlon or running event
Dance every day — whether you're good at it or not
Teach yourself to handstand
Do 10,000 steps a day
Try a home workout
Go for morning walks in silence
Try yoga
Cycle to work
Go on a 30 day bike ride and see how far you get
Take up a new exercise or martial art you can learn from YouTube
Spend time upside down or with your legs up the wall

Finance (p97)

Recycle your stuff
Only buy things with cash
Ditch mainstream products
Find a good money management app
Double what you save each day
Share with your neighbours
Put your pennies in a jar
Can you turn £100 into £500 in a month or £500 into £5000?
Stop wasting your food
Live on a strict budget for a month then splash out at the end
Start saving 10% of your income and love doing it
Sell 30 things you don't need, use or wear anymore and see how much money you make at the end of the month
Reflect on your attitude towards money
Learn more about money through James Altucher

Be generous with your money

Giving up challenges (p46)
Sending unfriendly emails
Offloading onto others
Giving people your advice when it's unasked for
Being a people pleaser
Waiting around for the 'right' time
Comparing yourself obsessively to others
Your grudges
Watching TV
Your phone
Resisting stuff
Blaming everyone and everything
Being horrible to yourself
Something you've been wanting to give up for a long time

Home life (p84)
Give your home a complete spring clean
Start an upcycling project for your home
Leave nice surprise notes in your home
Install a blackboard for messages
Pay attention when doing everyday tasks
Fix broken stuff in your home
Live with limited material items
Rent your home with Airbnb
Stop eating meals in front of the TV
Select new images for your home
Collect interesting rocks for your garden or home
Choose a different cupboard or drawer in your home to
organise
Give away one thing a day that you don't need
Make natural products for your home
Feng Shui all rooms in your home

Keep your bed nicely made
Learn how to fix your car
Revamp your garden
Make a small pond
Make a wormery or insect hotel for your garden
Make a home photo board
Make your bedroom a technology free zone
Create a space in your home for meditation and relaxation
Get a SAD lamp
Light candles
Make art for your walls
Fill your home with more plants
Start a fire wood log collection
Always recycle and compost food waste
Make a note of how much time you spend doing different everyday activities
Mend old clothes
Stop buying bottled water
Organise everything you need the day before
Collect interesting objects to grow plants in
Keep a folder of food recipes
Make sure your house is tidy when you return home
Hide all clutter

Inner life and meditation (p49)

Try the OSHO Nataraj meditation
Try the eye wandering exercise
Make your hobby your meditation
Spend five minutes focusing on your breath
Practise alternate nostril breathing to feel more balanced
Try body scan meditations
Music meditation
Try different chakra meditations
Dance like noone is watching
Incorporate the four paths of yoga into your life
Live by the 8 Limbs of Yoga

Practise body tapping techniques to prepare you for meditation
Get the Headspace App if you're new to meditation
Practise heart based meditation practices to let go of emotional baggage
Practise Buddhist Loving and Kindness meditations
Practise the Brahmari or the humming bee breath exercise
Practise the imagination wandering exercise
Practise Kapalbhati breathing to make your head glow
Practise Breath of Fire
Go on a local pilgrimage
Practise mantra meditation
Meditate with singing bowls
Meditate at 4am
Practise meditating in your dreams
Practise everyday mindfulness
Try object meditation
Try meditating with prayer beads
Try 5Rhythms
Reflect on the question who am I?
Practise yoga nidra
Spend each day being as 'present' as possible and absorbed in everything you do
Try a themed mood challenge

Jobs, work, and career boosting (p94)

Learn copywriting
Offer your services on Freelance sites
Start teaching something you're good at
Write a nonfiction or fiction ebook
Get work experience
Talk to people who can help with your career
Learn new skills on Lynda
What's the one thing you'd do every day for free? Write down steps and ideas for accomplishing it.
Start an Etsy Shop

Buy a plant and hang nice quotes on it
Offer to do social media and digital marketing for companies
Grow fruit/veg in your office
Do lunchtime fitness sessions

Kindness to yourself, others, and the environment (p125)

Give back to the planet
Show others your true self
Give up your seat if you commute by train
Buy homeless people hot drinks
Send a postcard to an old friend
Give a compliment a day
Give useful ideas to people
Volunteer for a cause you believe in
Give people good hugs
Write nice/ funny made up horoscopes for people
Give away books you no longer need
Write out and do 30 different random acts of kindness
Get involved with or start a local activist group
Do karma yoga (selfless service) for at least 15 mins a day
Spend 30 days fundraising for a charity or cause of your choice
Write down something you love about your partner every day and give them the list after your month is up
Make someone a 30 song playlist
Don't check your phone when you're with people
Look after other people's pets while they're away
Send appreciation notes and tweets
Speak kindly about people
Give people your full attention
Thank, tip or give small presents to people who aren't expecting it
Treat everyone with the same respect
Be the one to end gossipy conversations
Leave food in your garden for birds

Get to know your neighbours
Introduce your friends/ acquaintances/ contacts to one another
See the good in people
Give away some of your things for free
Try WWOOFING
Switch cynicism for skepticism
Try tithing
Make decisions from your inner self not ego
Be a person of action *and* words
Remember little things people say
Be a humble person
Leave a note for a stranger to discover

Logic and memory (113)

Do sudoku or crosswords
Play brain games on Lumosity
Improve your memory with chunking
Play chess
Put a jigsaw together
Answer general knowledge questions
Solve IQ questions
Get better at object perception by throwing stuff
Memorise countries and/ or capital cities
Memorise past presidents/ prime ministers from your country
Memorise Greek gods and goddesses

Manifesting and the law of attraction (p44)

Make an image board
Reflect on the Law of Attraction
Practise creative visualisation
Practise manifesting small things
Write yourself a cheque

Be grateful for everything you have

Note to you (p8)

Original 30 day challenge list of 100 ideas from my blog (p135)

Productivity at work (p91)

Write out your three most important tasks for the day
Check your emails only twice a day
Go meeting free for a month
No work related conversations after work hours
No office gossiping
Tackle your most important tasks first
Come into work half an hour early
Ditch working over-time
Quit complaining at work
Fill your office with more plants
Practise meditating with your colleagues
Limit social media use (unless it's your job)
Try out the Pomodoro Technique by breaking your day into 25 min slots
Give up multitasking

Questions (30 thought provoking questions for 30 days)

Who are you?
Which fictional character would you be and why?
Do you believe in a God or a higher power? If so, why or why not?
What would you do without fear?
If you could be an animal for a day, what would you choose and why?
What and who inspires you?

If you could spread one message or good idea, what would it be?

What do you spend most of your time thinking about?

What have been your happiest moments in life?

Is it possible to get rid of the ego?

What is the universe?

Is reincarnation possible?

How might you make the world a more peaceful place?

What lies behind the mind?

What's the one thing you've been putting off? Do it today.

If you're not your thoughts, things, interests, opinions, what are you?

If you had to change one thing about yourself (if anything) today, what might it be?

What is love?

What excites you?

What can you do today to help others more?

Will science eventually explain everything?

What happens when a person dies?

When and why did religion begin?

Where would you like to be in five years' time

Imagine being at your own funeral. What might people say about you?

What is the secret to a lasting relationship?

What is past present and future?

Is it possible for love to last forever?

How would you live your life or what would you do differently if no one was judging you?

What are you going to do today to be kind to yourself?

Recreation and fun (p76)

Play more

Create a bucket list of 30 things in 30 days

Create or work on your blog

Watch documentaries

Become a master of magic

Switch your daily newspaper for a specialist magazine
Make yourself and other people laugh
Play one good song a day first thing in the morning
Make your own beer, wine or sloe gin
Look at the stars
Press flowers
Learn numerology
Get an allotment or grow veg in your garden
Make a family tree
Learn graphology
Build a luxury permanent den in your garden
Learn henna tattooing
See how far you can get hitchhiking
Design a treasure hunt
Read a different newspaper
Listen to a new podcast a day
Learn origami
Laminate
Plant a flower a day — in your garden or just in random places
Start bird watching
Create themed playlists
Watch the sunrise
Write out random directions to see where you end up
Live like a tourist in your home city
Go foraging
Teach your dog new tricks
Walk slowly in busy places
Play with Lego
Listen to songs from your youth
Visit local tourist destinations in your area and do what's opposite

Self improvement misc (p34)
Keep a thought journal
Do something out of your comfort zone

Celebrate small accomplishments
Write down nagging thoughts on paper and thrown them away
Keep a general diary or journal
Practise laughter yoga, also known as hasya yoga
Start that project you've been meaning to do for ages
Write a letter or 30 line poem to your future self
Believe in magic
Create a new daily routine for yourself
Start a happiness journal
Ask people what your strengths and weaknesses are
Take note of the excuses you make
Learn to read body language
Plan your outfits the day before
Be really tidy
Spend less time on household chores
Develop your emotional intelligence
Question advice you're given
Speak or listen more
Show your vulnerable side
Develop your common sense and ability to plan ahead
Ditch your common sense
See life through an artist's eye
Take time out each day to watch your thoughts play out like a film
Be totally honest — so no lying for 30 days
Care less what other people think about you
Take more notice of what others think of you
Refrain from giving your opinion
Give your opinion more
Create affirmations for your life
Write down a positive thought first thing in the morning
Write down ideas for accomplishing a long term goal
Do one thing each day that makes you feel inspired
Spend each day being as 'present' as possible
Spend time in nature
Spend time with animals

Make positive subliminal messages for your computer or mirror
Decide to become a master at something
Develop your introverted or extroverted side
Don't spread your energy over too many different things
Bring more variety into your life
Spend time alone
Don't judge yourself for feeling a certain way
Do nothing for 30 minutes a day
Question yourself when you meet someone you don't like
Trust your intuition and listen to your heart

Social and relationships (p120)

Speak to someone new
Eat with people you care about
Be more assertive
Strike up a conversation with a stranger while you're waiting for something
Hold eye contact with a stranger for longer than five seconds
Befriend someone on the bus or train
Remember the names of new people
Improve your conversational skills
Take it in turns to cook
Eat together at the dinner table
Treat everyone you meet as a potential new friend
Talk less. Listen more
Talk more
Teach yourself to get good at public speaking
Spend time with people you like
Seek to understand others' motives
Be completely selfless in your relationship
Give your partner space
Write out 30 questions each with your partner
Switch roles in your relationship
Swap hobbies with someone
Write your own personal relationship 30 day challenge

Technology, science, and mathematics (p110)

Learn anatomy through drawing the body
Use the Khan Academy
Read about multiverse theories
Teach yourself economics
Teach yourself basic Maths
Use the Brain and/or Anatomy Colouring Book
Learn about prominent scientists throughout history
Take things apart and put them back together
Build yourself a computer
Learn the periodic table
Solve a maths problem
Teach yourself basic computer programming
Keep a notebook of invention ideas
Reflect on consciousness
Learn about different kinds of renewable energy
Research the placebo effect
Design a simple app

Upcycling, crafts, and textiles (p70)

Make an item of clothing
Make sculptures from old hardback books
Collect travel tickets and make a collage
Draw on maps and frame them
Make a patchwork throw with 30 squares
Knit a scarf doing a few lines a day
Create a textile wall hanging
Make a weaving from found tree branches
Customise old clothes
Make a scrap fabric rug
Make paper stencil lanterns
Make cushion covers
Make jewellery

Learn bookbinding
Make bleach paint t-shirts
Upcycle your scrabble letters
Collect together 20 random objects. What can you make in a month?
Make handbags, purses and laptop cases from old hardback books
Knit a plastic bag shopping bag
Paint patterns on old shoes and bags
Make a board game
Upcycle furniture with newspaper, magazines, sheet music and comics
Make a mosaic table top or frame
Do up an old bike
Decorate stones
Make a piece of furniture

Video, music, media art and photography (p67)

Take a photo a day on your way to work
Teach yourself Photoshop, InDesign and Illustrator
Teach yourself photography
Sell a photograph a day
Photograph one beautiful thing every day
Choose a photography theme
Teach yourself to play a new instrument
Make a musical instrument
Learn how to read music
Learn to play music through feeling and intuition
Sing
Make a documentary or video
Create an online course
Teach yourself video editing
Record your own guided meditations
Film the progress of your 30 day challenge

Writing (p64)

Write a book in 30 days
Write a blog post a day
Write a themed poem a day
Write a series of personalised A-Z guides
Keep an 'everyday' travel journal
Write a poem by selecting words from the dictionary at random
Write a song
Create your own cookbook in a month or food blog
Be a journalist
Keep an ideas book for 30 days
Take a notebook with you everywhere
Write down things that made you laugh
Try free writing
Learn calligraphy
Make a quote jar

X (no challenges listed)

Your FREE 30 day challenge planner chart

Go to goo.gl/BbGBjp

Zzz sleep (p30)

Think only good thoughts straight before bed
Go to bed at 10pm and wake up at 6am
Train yourself to lucid dream
Keep a dream diary
Monitor your sleep
Try out sleeping with siestas
No computer or mobile phone screens after sunset
Go snooze free on your alarm
Turn your electronical devices off before bed
Place lavender under your pillow

Get yourself into a bedtime routine
Eat something or don't eat something before bed
Read something that makes your feel good before you go to sleep

~~The End~~ The beginning of your 30 day challenge

Finally, I want to thank you for buying and reading this book. I really appreciate it and I hope it's something you can continue using for years to come.

I hope you get everything you want and more from the 30 day challenges you choose to do and that they bring you joy, happiness, more balance, and something to look forward to in your day-to-day life. If you haven't already, don't forget you can download and print out your free 30 day challenge planner chart to help you track and document your progress. Use the link below.

Free 30 day challenge planner chart: goo.gl/BbGBjp

I'm also open to any suggestions you might have for improving this book. You can email me directly at Clare@thoughtbrick.com. I'd also love to hear how you get on with any of the 30 day challenges.

Write a review on Amazon for this book

If you think others would benefit from this book, I would be so grateful if you could write a review on Amazon sharing your thoughts about the book and/ or how your 30 day challenges are going.

Author Bio

Hi, I'm Clare Hudson, and I'm a yoga teacher and blogger based in London, but from Hull. Over the last four years, I've been taking steps towards creating a life that I love living and doing work that inspires me. 30 day challenges are still a big part of this.

I won't bore you with my life story, but read on if you want to know a bit more...

I have a degree in Fine Art and would love to do a Master's one day in either the history of yoga and meditation or transpersonal psychology. I never want to stop learning.

After years of not making any art, I recently set up an Etsy art shop with my Mum called Yoga Spirit Art, thanks to being inspired by a 30 day mandala drawing challenge that I did.

I've travelled quite a bit, lived on the Arctic Circle for half a year and have done a lot of different jobs before deciding to teach yoga, blog and build a life that makes me feel present and alive.

What I believe in and love to write about

I've read too many contradicting books and met so many interesting people to live fully by any one belief system. What works for one person might not work for someone else which is why these challenges are all so varied. It's up to you to decide what's right for you. Ultimately though, I believe in the power of thought, being connected to your heart and living out of love.

I set my blog Thought Brick up in 2013 with the help of my

brother Mike from Van Dog Traveller, after discovering an old book belonging to my grandparents, with the words Thought Brick handwritten inside. My grandparents used to use the term to highlight how powerful our thoughts are and that if you change your thoughts, you can change your life.

And on that note, I'd like to leave you with this quote by Lao Tzu.

"Watch your thoughts, for they become words.
Watch your words, for they become actions.
Watch your action, for they become habits.
Watch your habits, for they become character.
Watch your character, it becomes your destiny."
— Lao Tzu

End Notes

[1] Lally, P., van Jaarsveld, C.H.M., Potts, H.W.W. and Wardle, J. (2009) 'How are habits formed: Modelling habit formation in the real world', *European Journal of Social Psychology*, 40(6), pp. 998–1009. doi: 10.1002/ejsp.674.

[2] Barrett, P. (2012). How to do A handstand: From the basic exercises to the free standing handstand Pushup. North Charleston: CreateSpace.

[3] Fitbit. (2016). Fitbit official site for activity Trackers and more. Available at: https://www.fitbit.com/uk

[4] Choices, N. (2016, August 26). The 10, 000 steps challenge. Available at: http://www.nhs.uk/Livewell/loseweight/Pages/10000stepsc hallenge.aspx

[5] Publishing, C. B. (2007, August 28). Benefits of inversions. Available at: Yoga Poses, http://www.yogajournal.com/article/practice-section/everybody-upside-down/

[6] Publishing, C. B. (2007, August 28). Legs-up-the-wall pose - Viparita Karani - yoga pose. Available at: Beginners' Yoga Poses, http://www.yogajournal.com/pose/legs-up-the-wall-pose/

[7] Ajaou, H. Thevenet, F (2006). Discovering the Spices of Morocco. Casablanca: Editions Le Fennec.

[8] M, S., A, G., A, F.-L., & PMC, E. (1996). In vivo antioxidant effect of green and black tea in man. European Journal of Clinical Nutrition, 50(1), 28–32. Available at: http://europepmc.org/abstract/MED/8617188

[9] Choices, N. (2016, August 26). Top diets review for 2016. Retrieved from http://www.nhs.uk/Livewell/loseweight/Pages/top-10-most-popular-diets-review.aspx

[10] Axe, J. (2014, February 17). 7 reasons to drink Kombucha everyday. Available at: Digestive Health, https://draxe.com/7-reasons-drink-kombucha-everyday/

[11] Fleming, A. (2013, February 26). Healthy food: Can you train yourself to like it? The Guardian. Available at: https://www.theguardian.com/lifeandstyle/wordofmouth/2013/feb/26/healthy-food-train-yourself-like-it

[12] Choices, N. (2016, March 17). Why 5 A DAY? Available at: http://www.nhs.uk/Livewell/5ADAY/Pages/Why5ADAY.aspx

[13] McNight, C. (2015, April 23). Benefits of garlic & ginger. Available at: Livestrong, http://www.livestrong.com/article/250817-benefits-of-garlic-ginger/

[14] Mercola, J. (2015, December 12). Chewing food thoroughly is the First step to healthy digestion. Available at: Mercola, http://articles.mercola.com/sites/articles/archive/2015/12/12/chewing-food-thoroughly.aspx

[15] Mariaca, K. (2015, April 2). Benefits of facial steam. Available at: Livestrong, http://www.livestrong.com/article/114247-benefits-facial-steam/

[16] Borreli, L. (2014, June 24). I tried A Cryotherapy chamber. Healthy Living. Available at: http://www.medicaldaily.com/benefits-cold-showers-7-

reasons-why-taking-cool-showers-good-your-health-289524

[17] Oskia Skincare, London. (2016). Available at: Oskia Skincare Ltd, https://www.oskiaskincare.com/beauty-bible/eyemassageroutine/

[18] Hoffman, K. (2015) *Is natural deodorant better? I tried an aluminum-free product for A week, and it Wasn't the pits.* Available at: https://www.bustle.com/articles/75143-is-natural-deodorant-better-i-tried-an-aluminum-free-product-for-a-week-and-it-wasnt-the

[19] Crocker, N. (2012, May 29). The Tiny Guide to creating the Flossing habit: Zen habits. Available at: Zen Habits, https://zenhabits.net/floss/

[20] Douillard, J. (2016, October 13). The Truth About Oil Pulling Ayurvedic Health. Available at: from Life Spa, http://lifespa.com/the-truth-about-oil-pulling/

[21] Korb, A. (2012, August). Smile: A powerful tool. Available at: Psychology Today, https://www.psychologytoday.com/blog/prefrontal-nudity/201208/smile-powerful-tool

[22] Ober, C., Sinatra, S. T., & Zucker, M. (2010). *Earthing: The most important health discovery ever?* United States: Basic Health Publications.

[23] Introducing dream Sculpting by Andrew Holecek. Available at: http://courses.mindvalleyacademy.com/dream-sculpting/special?utm_source=aff

[24] LaBerge, S., & Rheingold, H. (1997). Exploring the world of lucid dreaming. New York: Random House Publishing Group.

[25] How do I track my sleep? (2016, October 28). Available at: Fitbit Inc,
https://help.fitbit.com/articles/en_US/Help_article/1314
[26] Hegarty, S. (2012) *The myth of the eight-hour sleep.* Available at: http://www.bbc.co.uk/news/magazine-16964783

[27] Sample, I. (2013, May 22). Peering at bright screens after dark could harm health, doctor claims. Available at: The Guardian,
https://www.theguardian.com/science/2013/may/22/peering-bright-screens-dark-harm-health

[28] Electronics in the bedroom: Why it's necessary to turn off before you tuck in. (2016). Retrieved from National Sleep Foundation, https://sleepfoundation.org/ask-the-expert/electronics-the-bedroom

[29] Lavender. (1997). Available at: University of Maryland Medical Centre,
http://umm.edu/health/medical/altmed/herb/lavender

[30] Jones, T. (2016, October 28). Is it a bad idea to eat before bed? The surprising truth. Available at: Authority Nutrition, https://authoritynutrition.com/eating-before-bed/

[31] Goleman, D. (1996). Emotional intelligence: Why it can matter more than IQ. London: Bloomsbury Publishing PLC.

[32] Brown, B. (2010, December 23). The power of vulnerability. Available at:
https://www.ted.com/talks/brene_brown_on_vulnerability

[33] Williams, R. (2013). Do self-affirmations work? A revisit. Available at: Psychology Today,
https://www.psychologytoday.com/blog/wired-

success/201305/do-self-affirmations-work-revisit

[34] TED: Ideas worth spreading. Available at: TED Conferences, https://www.ted.com/

[35] Gladwell, M. (2011). *Outliers: The story of success*. New York: Little, Brown & Company.

[36] Price, D. (2015, December 9). The 10,000 hour rule is wrong. How to really master a skill. Available at: http://www.makeuseof.com/tag/10000-hour-rule-wrong-really-master-skill/

[37] Cain, S. (2013). *Quiet: The power of introverts in a world that can't stop talking*. New York: Crown Publishing Group.

[38] Byrne, R. (2006). *The secret*. London: Simon & Schuster.

[39] Grout, P. (2013). *E-squared: Nine do-it-yourself energy experiments that prove your thoughts create your reality* (2nd ed.). Carlsbad, CA: Hay House Insights.

[40] Hudson, C. (2015) 'Vipassana Meditation — my 10 days in a silent retreat', Thought Brick, 4 September. Available at: http://thoughtbrick.com/meditation/vipassana-meditation-10-days-silent-retreat-2/.

[41] Lally, P., van Jaarsveld, C.H.M., Potts, H.W.W. and Wardle, J. (2009) 'How are habits formed: Modelling habit formation in the real world', *European Journal of Social Psychology*, 40(6), pp. 998–1009. doi: 10.1002/ejsp.674.

[42] *OSHO Nataraj meditation* (2016) Available at: http://www.osho.com/meditate/active-meditations/nataraj-meditation.

[43] Vishnudevananda, S. (2008) *Hatha Yoga Pradipika*.

Motilal Banarsidass Publishers.

[44] gosho2212 (2011) 03 - *Russill Paul - Bija mantras.mp4*.
Available at: https://www.youtube.com/watch?v=Z-mkOgTSzqw.
[45] *Shakti Dance* (2016) Available at:
http://www.shaktidance.co.uk/.

[46] Satyam, B., Mithya, J. and Parah, J.B.N. (no date)
Sivananda yoga Vedanta Centres. Available at:
http://www.sivananda.org/teachings/fourpaths.html.

[47] Satchidananda, S. (2015) *The yoga Sutras of Patanjali-Integral yoga pocket edition: Translation and commentary by Sri swami Satchidananda*. Integral Yoga Publications.

[48] *Emotional freedom technique (EFT) - emotional health* (1997) Available at: http://eft.mercola.com

[49] *Get some Headspace* (2016) Available at:
https://www.headspace.com/

[50] *Open heart meditation benefits* (no date) Available at:
http://www.lotuscentre.org/index.php/2015-03-29-14-53-45/open-heart-meditation-benefits.

[51] A basic Buddhism guide: Loving-kindness meditation ,
by Ven. Pannyavaro (1996) Available at:
http://www.buddhanet.net/e-learning/loving-kindness.htm.

[52] Vishnudevananda, S. (2008) *Hatha Yoga Pradipika*.
Motilal Banarsidass Publishers.

[53] Jeffers, S. (1987) *Feel the fear and do it anyway:
Dynamic techniques for turning fear, indecision, and anger into power, action, and love*. San Diego: Harcourt Brace Jovanovich.

[54] *Sivananda yoga Vedanta Centres and Ashrams* (no date) Available at: http://www.sivananda.org/.

[55] Breath of fire, Kundalini yoga (2009) Available at: http://www.kundalini-yoga-info.com/breath-of-fire.html#.WFKMt6KLRbU.

[56] Introducing dream Sculpting by Andrew Holecek (no date) Available at: http://courses.mindvalleyacademy.com/dream-sculpting/special?utm_source=aff.

[57] 5Rhythms (2016) Available at: https://www.5rhythms.com/.

[58] Godman, D., Maharshi, S. and Ramana, M. (1988) *Be as you are: The teachings of Sri Ramana Maharshi.* New Delhi: Penguin Group (USA).

[59] *Richard Miller, Ph.D* (2016) Available at: https://www.scienceandnonduality.com/speakers/richard-miller-ph-d/.

[60] *Tate Artists Mark Rothko* (no date) Available at: http://www.tate.org.uk/art/artists/mark-rothko-1875.

[61] *Howard Hodgkin* (2015) Available at: https://howard-hodgkin.com/.

[62] *Andy Goldsworthy* (2016) Available at: http://www.artnet.com/artists/andy-goldsworthy/.

[63] *Tate Artists Jackson Pollock* (1912-1956) (no date) Available at: http://www.tate.org.uk/art/artists/jackson-pollock-1785.

[64] *National novel writing month* (1999) Available at:

http://nanowrimo.org/.

[65] *Thomas Truax* (no date) Available at:
https://www.thomastruax.com/instruments/.

[66] *Tate Artists Kurt Schwitters* (1887-1948) (no date)
Available at: http://www.tate.org.uk/art/artists/kurt-
schwitters-1912.
[67] *Hitchhiker's safety* (no date) Available at:
http://hitchwiki.org/en/Hitchhiker%27s_safety

[68] Sawaya, N. (2003) *Brickartist*. Available at:
http://www.brickartist.com/.

[69] *What is SAD?* (no date) Available at:
http://www.sad.org.uk/.

[70] Nield, D. (2016) *These are the best Houseplants to
improve indoor air quality, study finds.* Available at:
http://www.sciencealert.com/the-right-houseplants-could-
improve-indoor-air-quality-researchers-say.

[71] Hudson, C. (2015) 'The results of my Regus Productivity
Challenge', *Thought Brick*, 23 December. Available at:
http://thoughtbrick.com/lifestyle/the-results-of-my-regus-
productivity-challenge/.

[72] Ferriss, T. (2008) *The 4-Hour work week*. London: Ebury
Publishing.

[73] Keller, G. and Papasan, J. (2013) *The one thing: The
surprisingly simple truth behind extraordinary results.*
Austin, TX: Bard Press TX.

[74] Russell, H. (2016) *Why the Danes finish work on time,
every single day.* Available at:
http://www.stylist.co.uk/life/living-danishly-how-and-why-to-
leave-work-on-time-every-single-day-job-careers-work-life-

balance-happiness.

[75] Cummings, T. (no date) The Pomodoro technique: Is it right for you? Available at:
http://www.lifehack.org/articles/productivity/the-pomodoro-technique-is-it-right-for-you.html.

[76] Scott, S. (2014) *How to Write a Nonfiction eBook in 21 Days - That Readers LOVE!*
[77] WRAP (no date) *Love Food hate waste* homepage. Available at: https://www.lovefoodhatewaste.com/

[78] Altucher, J. (2013) *Choose Yourself.*

[79] Little, S. (2004) *Isms: Understanding art*. London: A & C Black Publishers.

[80] De Bono, E. (2000) *Six thinking hats*. London: Penguin Books.

[81] *Howard Gardner, multiple intelligences and education* (2013) Available at: http://infed.org/mobi/howard-gardner-multiple-intelligences-and-education/.

[82] Taggart, C. (2015) *500 Words You Should Know*. Michael O'Mara.

[83] Diamond, M.C.C., Scheibel, A.B. and Elson, L.M. (1985) *The human brain coloring book*. New York: HarperCollins Publishers.

[84] Don Johnson (2007) Tom Lehrer *CHEMISTRY element song*. Available at:

https://www.youtube.com/watch?v=DYW50F42ss8
[85] O'Danu, M. (2014) *Play, don't replay! HELP PREVENT PTSD*. Available at:

https://janemcgonigal.com/2014/03/27/help-prevent-ptsd/.

[86] McLeod, S. (2009) *Short term memory.* Available at: http://www.simplypsychology.org/short-term-memory.html

23318077R00107

Made in the USA
San Bernardino, CA
23 January 2019